Southern Living
big book of
slow cooking

200 fresh, wholesome recipes—ready and waiting

Hard Cover:
ISBN-13: 978-0-8487-3976-8
ISBN-10: 0-8487-3976-0

Soft Cover:
ISBN-13: 978-0-8487-3701-6
ISBN-10: 0-8487-3701-6
Library of Congress Control Number: 2012942499

Printed in the United States of America
First Printing 2012

Oxmoor House

VP, Publishing Director: Jim Childs
Editorial Director: Leah McLaughlin
Creative Director: Felicity Keane
Senior Brand Manager: Daniel Fagan
Senior Editor: Rebecca Brennan
Managing Editor: Rebecca Benton

Southern Living® Big Book of Slow Cooking

Editor: Susan Hernandez Ray
Project Editors: Emily Chappell, Megan McSwain Yeatts
Assistant Designer: Allison Sperando Potter
Director, Test Kitchen: Elizabeth Tyler Austin
Assistant Directors, Test Kitchen: Julie Christopher, Julie Gunter
Recipe Developers and Testers: Wendy Ball, R.D.; Victoria E. Cox; Stefanie Maloney; Callie Nash; Leah Van Deren
Recipe Editor: Alyson Moreland Haynes
Food Stylists: Margaret Monroe Dickey, Catherine Crowell Steele
Photography Director: Jim Bathie
Senior Photo Stylist: Kay E. Clarke
Photo Stylist: Katherine Eckert Coyne
Assistant Photo Stylist: Mary Louise Menendez
Senior Production Manager: Greg A. Amason

Contributors

Project Editor: Allyson Angle
Recipe Developers and Testers: Tamara Goldis, Erica Hopper, Tonya Johnson, Kyra Moncrief, Kathleen Royal Phillips
Copy Editor: Kate Johnson, Barry Wise Smith
Proofreaders: Julie Bosche, Lauren Brooks, Mary Ann Laurens
Indexer: Nanette Cardon
Interns: Morgan Bolling; Mackenzie Cogle; Jessica Cox, R.D.; Laura Hoxworth; Susan Kemp; Alicia Lavender; Anna Pollock; Emily Robinson; Ashley White

Southern Living®

Editor: M. Lindsay Bierman
Creative Director: Robert Perino
Managing Editor: Candace Higginbotham
Executive Editors: Rachel Hardage, Jessica S. Thuston
Food Director: Shannon Sliter Satterwhite
Test Kitchen Director: Rebecca Kracke Gordon
Senior Writer: Donna Florio
Senior Food Editor: Mary Allen Perry
Recipe Editor: JoAnn Weatherly
Assistant Recipe Editor: Ashley Arthur
Test Kitchen Professionals: Norman King, Pam Lolley, Angela Sellers
Senior Photographers: Ralph Lee Anderson, Gary Clark, Art Meripol
Photographers: Robbie Caponetto, Laurey W. Glenn
Photo Research Coordinator: Ginny P. Allen
Senior Photo Stylist: Buffy Hargett
Editorial Assistant: Pat York

Time Home Entertainment Inc.

Publisher: Richard Fraiman
VP, Strategy & Business Development: Steven Sandonato
Executive Director, Marketing Services: Carol Pittard
Executive Director, Retail & Special Sales: Tom Mifsud
Director, Bookazine Development & Marketing: Laura Adam
Publishing Director: Joy Butts
Finance Director: Glenn Buonocore
Assistant General Counsel: Helen Wan

To order additional publications, call
1-800-765-6400 or 1-800-491-0551.

For more books to enrich your life,
visit oxmoorhouse.com.

To search, savor, and share thousands
of recipes, visit myrecipes.com.

Cover: Spicy Asian Barbecued Drummettes, page 246

Contents

Welcome

The slow cooker—once a novelty kitchen gadget that collected dust on many a countertop—has now become **an essential appliance** for beginner cooks, seasoned chefs, party hosts, and anyone who wants to savor the flavor of delicious dishes without spending countless hours in the kitchen. Throughout these pages you'll find a variety of recipes you can prepare with little prep time and a lot less effort than with your standard approach to cooking. We start with our best Test Kitchen tips so that, though cook time may be slow, preparation and cleanup can be quick and simple.

Reminisce through chapters of nostalgic dishes, including classic favorites like **Collard Greens** (page 24) and **"Cowboy" Pot Roast** (page 45). Even casseroles take on new meaning—just mix the ingredients for **Spaghetti Casserole** (page 50) in the afternoon, let your slow cooker do the work, and supper's ready.

But supper isn't the only reason to get excited. Flip to our **"Yes, You Can Make *That* in Your Slow Cooker"** chapter (page 10), and you'll be amazed at what you can accomplish—from salty **boiled peanuts** (page 13) to warm, melt-in-your-mouth **carrot cake** (page 20). In fact, some things are just better in a slow cooker. Our **Chocolate–Peanut Butter Cheesecake** (page 21) recipe creates a creamy, smooth texture that only the slow cooker can achieve with its ability to lock in moisture.

Planning a party? Entertain a crowd by using your slow cooker for easy access—entrées, appetizers, and desserts will be ready and waiting when guests arrive. We've even included some deliciously fragrant beverages to keep your guests warm and toasty when it's cold out. Try our **Extreme Hot Chocolate** (page 131) and **Caramel Apple Cider** (page 133) for sweet, slow-cooked comfort that won't need reheating.

Whatever the occasion, the Southern Living *Big Book of Slow Cooking* offers something for everyone, and your time can be spent enjoying the company.

Cheers!

Shannon

Shannon Satterwhite

Slow-Cooker School

A slow cooker is a cook's best friend. With so many on the market, it's hard to know what to buy. Here are some tips to help you get started:

Size wise. The first thing to consider when selecting a slow cooker is which size best suits your family. If you are cooking for a family of 1 or 2, then a 3- or 4-qt. size should work for you. Families of 4 or larger should look at a 5- or 6-qt. slow cooker. Or, if you love to have leftovers, then a 6-qt. cooker is a good selection.

Keep a lid on it. A snug-fitting, see-through lid works best. Removing the lid during cooking releases a great deal of heat, so you want to be able to see your food through the lid rather than having to lift it.

Removable inserts. Slow cookers with removable inserts are easier to clean than one-piece units. Depending on the manufacturer, the insert may be dishwasher safe. Some of these inserts can go from the freezer to the cooker, and some can even be used to brown meat on the cooktop before slow cooking.

It's all in the timing. Many slow cookers come with programmable timers. This is an especially nice feature if you will be gone all day. If your slow cooker doesn't have one, you can purchase an external timer. Simply plug the external slow-cooker timer into the wall outlet, and then plug the cooker into the timer. It allows you to set your cooking time; when that time has expired, the timer automatically switches the cooker to warm.

Follow our Test Kitchen's best tricks:

1.Make-ahead magic. If your slow cooker has a removable insert, you can assemble the ingredients in the insert the night before for some recipes, and then refrigerate the whole thing. Keep in mind that starting with cold ingredients may increase the cook time.

2. Don't get burned. Although cooking time is more flexible in a slow cooker than in an oven, overcooking is possible, so test for doneness close to the time given in the recipe.

3. Safe travels. If you're taking a slow-cooker dish to grandmother's house, you may want to invest in a model that features a locking top and an insulated carrying case. Or you can attach heavy-duty rubber bands around the handles and lid, and then wrap the slow cooker in towels or newspaper. (See image below.)

4. Remember time conversions. One hour on HIGH equals approximately 2 hours on LOW.

5. Cut uniform pieces. When cutting meat or vegetables, be sure pieces are the same size so they cook evenly.

6. Trim the fat. Slow cooking requires little fat. Trim excess fat and skin from meats and poultry.

7. Don't stir things up. There's no need to stir ingredients unless a recipe specifically calls for it. Just layer the ingredients as the recipe directs.

8. You won't need much liquid. Use only the amount of liquid specified in the recipe.

9. Lay it on thick. You can thicken the juices and make gravy by removing the lid and cooking on HIGH for the last 20 to 30 minutes.

10. Finish fresh. Add seasonings and garnishes to the dish once it comes out of the slow cooker to enhance the flavor.

Slow cooking is a safe method for preparing food if you follow these standard procedures:

1. Fill your slow cooker at least half full but no more than two-thirds full. This helps meat products reach a safe internal temperature quickly and cook evenly.

2. The U.S. Department of Agriculture recommends that you cook raw meat and poultry dishes on HIGH for the first hour to speed up the time it takes to reach a safe internal temperature. After the first hour, you can reduce the heat to LOW for the remainder of the cooking time, if desired.

3. If the recipe calls for browning the meat first, you can forgo the HIGH setting for the first hour. Precooking the meat increases the initial temperature of the ingredients, eliminating the safety risk associated with slow cooking raw meats.

4. Defrost any frozen foods before cooking a dish that includes meat, poultry, or seafood. This ensures that the contents of the insert reach a safe internal temperature quickly.

5. Don't use your slow cooker to reheat leftovers because it will not heat the food fast enough, resulting in an increased risk of bacterial contamination. Instead, use a microwave or cooktop.

Follow these tips for making cleaning the slow cooker a little easier:

1. Allow the slow-cooker insert to cool completely before washing it. Cold water poured over a hot insert can cause it to crack.

2. To minimize cleanup, buy clear, heavy-duty plastic liners made to fit 3- to 6½-qt. oval and round slow cookers. Place the plastic liner inside the slow cooker before adding the recipe ingredients. Then, serve the meal directly from the slow cooker, with the liner in place. Once the cooker has cooled, just throw away the plastic liner along with the mess.

3. If you don't have slow-cooker liners, be sure to spray the slow cooker with cooking spray before placing the food inside. This will make cleanup much easier.

Fruited Carrot Cake, page 20

Yes, You Can Make *That* in Your Slow Cooker

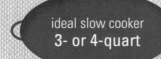
Caramelized Onions

makes 2 cups • hands-on time: 10 min. • total time: 4 hr., 10 min.

2   bacon slices
2   Tbsp. butter, melted
2   medium-size sweet onions, sliced
¼   tsp. salt
⅛   tsp. pepper

1. Cook bacon in skillet until crisp; remove bacon, reserving 1 Tbsp. drippings. Reserve bacon for another use.

2. Combine drippings, melted butter, and remaining ingredients in a 3- or 4-qt. slow cooker. Stir well to coat onions.

3. Cover and cook on HIGH 4 hours.

French Onion Soup: Stir 2 (10½-oz.) cans beef consommé and ¼ cup dry white wine into cooked onions in slow cooker. Cover and cook on HIGH 15 minutes or just until heated. Sprinkle with shredded Gruyère cheese and restaurant-style croutons. Makes 5 cups.

Sina's Georgia-Style Boiled Peanuts

makes 18 cups • hands-on time: 3 min. • total time: 18 hr., 3 min.

1½ lb. raw peanuts, in shell
¾ to 1 cup salt

1. Combine peanuts, salt, and 14 cups water in a tall, oval 6-qt. slow cooker. Cover and cook on HIGH 18 hours or until peanuts are soft. Drain peanuts before serving or storing. Store in zip-top plastic bags in refrigerator up to 2 weeks.

Cajun Boiled Peanuts: Add 1 (3-oz.) package boil-in-bag shrimp-and-crab boil and ⅓ to ½ cup hot sauce (we tested with Frank's) to slow cooker before cooking.

Tomato-Cranberry Chutney

makes 8 cups • hands-on time: 13 min. • total time: 10 hr., 13 min.

¼ cup butter
1 (8-oz.) container prechopped onion
1 tsp. salt
2 tsp. curry powder
1 tsp. jarred minced garlic
½ tsp. cayenne pepper
½ tsp. dry mustard
3 (14.5-oz.) cans stewed tomatoes, drained and coarsely chopped
1 cup unsweetened applesauce
1 cup malt vinegar
1 cup dried sweetened cranberries
½ cup sugar

1. Melt butter in a medium skillet over medium-high heat. Add onion; sauté until tender. Stir in salt and next 4 ingredients. Sauté 2 minutes.

2. Combine onion mixture, tomatoes, and remaining ingredients in a 3-qt. slow cooker. Cook, uncovered, on HIGH 10 hours or until thick, stirring after 5 hours.

3. Spoon into hot, sterilized jars; cover and store in refrigerator.

Note: We tested with Craisins Original Dried Cranberries.

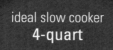
Spiced Sugarplum-Apple Butter

makes 3 cups • hands-on time: 10 min. • total time: 10 hr., 10 min.

2   cups dried pitted plums, chopped
4   medium Granny Smith apples,
     peeled and chopped
¼   cup apple cider or apple juice
¼   cup firmly packed light brown
     sugar
¼   cup honey
1   Tbsp. ground cinnamon
½   tsp. ground cloves
½   tsp. ground ginger
½   tsp. ground nutmeg

1. Stir together all ingredients in a 4-qt. slow cooker. Cover and cook on LOW 10 hours.

2. Stir until chunky. Spoon into hot, sterilized jars. Cover and cool completely; store in refrigerator up to 2 weeks.

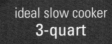

Three-Cheese Penne Bake

makes 6 servings • hands-on time: 6 min. • total time: 2 hr., 21 min.

12   oz. uncooked penne pasta
     (3½ cups)
1½   cups half-and-half
2   Tbsp. butter, melted
½   tsp. salt
¼   tsp. dry mustard
¼   tsp. ground red pepper
1   (12-oz.) can evaporated milk
1   cup (4 oz.) shredded Gruyère
     cheese
½   cup (2 oz.) freshly grated Parmesan
     cheese
½   cup (2 oz.) shredded American cheese
1½   cups soft fresh breadcrumbs
2   Tbsp. butter, melted
2   Tbsp. chopped fresh parsley

1. Cook pasta in boiling, salted water 6 minutes; drain. Spoon into a lightly greased 3-qt. slow cooker. Whisk together half-and-half and next 5 ingredients; stir in cheeses. Stir cheese mixture into pasta. Cover and cook on LOW 2 hours.

2. Stir pasta mixture. Cover and let stand 15 minutes.

3. Meanwhile, preheat oven to 400°. Toss together breadcrumbs and 2 Tbsp. melted butter. Spread crumb mixture on a baking sheet. Bake at 400° for 10 minutes or until toasted. Transfer crumbs to a bowl. Add parsley, and toss well. Sprinkle crumb mixture over pasta mixture. Serve immediately.

ideal slow cooker
6-quart

Lasagna

makes 6 servings • hands-on time: 15 min. • total time: 3 hr., 15 min.

1 (28-oz.) can diced tomatoes, drained

1 (28-oz.) jar chunky pasta sauce

3 garlic cloves, finely chopped

¼ cup fresh oregano, chopped

½ tsp. kosher salt

¾ tsp. pepper, divided

1 (16-oz.) container ricotta cheese

½ cup fresh flat-leaf parsley, chopped

½ cup (2 oz.) shredded Parmesan cheese

1 (12-oz.) package lasagna noodles

1 bunch Swiss chard, tough stems removed, torn into large pieces

3 cups (12 oz.) shredded mozzarella cheese

1. In a medium bowl, combine tomatoes, sauce, garlic, oregano, salt, and ½ tsp. pepper. In another medium bowl, combine ricotta, parsley, Parmesan cheese, and remaining ¼ tsp. pepper. Spoon ⅓ cup of tomato mixture into a 6-qt. slow cooker.

2. Top with a single layer of noodles, breaking them to fit as necessary. Add half the Swiss chard. Dollop with one-third of ricotta mixture and one-third of remaining tomato mixture. Sprinkle with one-third of mozzarella cheese. Add another layer of noodles and repeat with other ingredients. Finish with a layer of noodles and remaining ricotta mixture, tomato mixture, and mozzarella. Cover and cook on LOW 2 to 3 hours or until noodles are tender.

ideal slow cooker
6-quart oval

Ham-and-Swiss Quiche

makes 6 servings • hands-on time: 11 min. • total time: 3 hr., 16 min.

1 (14.1-oz.) package refrigerated piecrusts

2 cups (8 oz.) shredded Swiss cheese, divided

1 cup chopped lean ham

4 green onions, chopped

6 large eggs

1 cup whipping cream

¼ tsp. salt

¼ tsp. freshly ground pepper

⅛ tsp. ground nutmeg

1. Cut piecrusts in half. Press 3 piecrust halves into bottom and 2 inches up sides of a greased 6-qt. oval slow cooker, overlapping seams by ¼ inch. Reserve remaining piecrust half for another use.

2. Cover and cook on HIGH 1½ hours.

3. Sprinkle 1 cup cheese, ham, and green onions over crust. Whisk together eggs and next 4 ingredients; pour over ingredients in crust. Sprinkle remaining 1 cup cheese over egg mixture.

4. Cover and cook on HIGH 1½ hours or until filling is set. Uncover and let stand 5 minutes before serving. Cut quiche into wedges, and serve immediately.

ideal slow cooker
7-quart

Lowcountry Shrimp Boil

makes 6 servings • hands-on time: 4 min. • total time: 5 hr., 34 min.

12 small new potatoes (1¼ lb.)
1 (12-oz.) can beer
4 to 5 Tbsp. Old Bay seasoning
2 celery ribs, cut into 4-inch pieces
1 onion, quartered
2 lemons, halved
1 lb. kielbasa sausage, cut into 1-inch pieces
½ (12-ct.) package frozen corn on the cob (do not thaw)
2 lb. unpeeled, large raw shrimp
Cocktail sauce

1. Place potatoes in a 7-qt. slow cooker. Add 10 cups water, beer, and next three ingredients. Squeeze juice from lemon halves into mixture in slow cooker; add lemon halves to slow cooker. Cover and cook on LOW 3 hours.

2. Add sausage and corn. Cover and cook on LOW 2 hours. Add shrimp; stir gently. Cover and cook on HIGH 15 minutes or until shrimp turn pink. Turn off cooker; let stand 15 minutes. Drain. Serve with cocktail sauce.

ideal slow cooker
4-quart

Fruited Carrot Cake

makes 8 to 10 servings • hands-on time: 28 min. • total time: 5 hr., 3 min. • pictured on page 10

Parchment paper
2   cups all-purpose flour
1½ cups sugar
2   tsp. baking powder
½   tsp. salt
1   tsp. ground cinnamon
¼   tsp. ground nutmeg
1   cup vegetable oil
½   cup unsweetened applesauce
1   tsp. vanilla extract
2   large eggs, beaten
1½ cups finely shredded carrot
½   cup raisins
½   cup sweetened flaked coconut
1   (8-oz.) can crushed pineapple in
      juice, drained
Cream Cheese Frosting
2   Tbsp. chopped crystallized ginger

1. Heavily grease the insert of a 4-qt. slow cooker. Line bottom of insert with parchment paper. Stir together flour and next 5 ingredients in a large bowl; add oil and next 3 ingredients, stirring just until dry ingredients are moistened. Stir in carrot and next 3 ingredients. Pour batter into prepared slow cooker. Cover top of slow cooker with aluminum foil and secure lid. Cook on LOW 3 to 3½ hours.

2. Remove insert from slow cooker. Cool cake, covered, in insert on a wire rack 5 minutes. Remove cake from insert, and cool completely on wire rack about 1 hour.

3. Meanwhile, prepare Cream Cheese Frosting. Spread top and sides of cooled cake with frosting. Sprinkle with crystallized ginger.

Cream Cheese Frosting

makes about 2½ cups • hands-on time: 10 min. • total time: 10 min.

¼   cup butter, softened
1   tsp. vanilla extract
1   (8-oz.) package cream cheese,
      softened
2   cups powdered sugar

1. Beat all ingredients until creamy.

Chocolate-Peanut Butter Cheesecake

makes 8 servings • hands-on time: 19 min. • total time: 11 hr., 49 min. • pictured on back cover

Cheesecake cooked in a slow cooker delivers creamy results, thanks to the steamy nature of the slow cooker, which holds in moisture as food cooks.

15 cream-filled chocolate sandwich cookies, crushed (1½ cups)

¼ cup butter, melted

1 cup peanut butter morsels

1 cup semisweet chocolate morsels

2 (8-oz.) packages cream cheese, softened

1 (3-oz.) package cream cheese, softened

¾ cup sugar

¼ cup whipping cream

1 tsp. vanilla extract

3 eggs

1. Combine crushed cookies and melted butter in a medium bowl; stir well. Press crumb mixture into bottom and 1 inch up sides of a lightly greased 8-inch springform pan. Set aside.

2. Microwave peanut butter morsels in a microwave-safe bowl at HIGH 1 minute or until melted, stirring after 30 seconds. Microwave chocolate morsels in a microwave-safe bowl at HIGH 1 minute or until melted, stirring after 30 seconds.

3. Meanwhile, beat cream cheese and sugar at medium speed with an electric mixer until blended. Add whipping cream and vanilla, beating at low speed until well blended. Add eggs, 1 at a time, beating until yellow disappears after each addition.

4. Add half of cream cheese mixture to melted peanut butter morsels, stirring until blended. Add remaining cream cheese mixture to melted chocolate morsels, stirring until blended. Pour chocolate batter into prepared crust. Spoon peanut butter batter, by tablespoonfuls, over chocolate batter; gently swirl with a knife.

5. Pour water to a depth of ½ inch into a 6-qt. round slow cooker. Place small round wire rack in cooker. Place cheesecake on wire rack. Place 3 layers of paper towels across top of slow cooker; cover with lid. Cook on HIGH 2½ hours or until cheesecake is set.

6. Remove cheesecake from slow cooker; gently run a knife around edge of cheesecake to loosen. Cool completely in pan on a wire rack (about 1 hour). Cover and chill 8 hours.

7. To serve cheesecake, remove sides of pan. Place cheesecake on a serving platter.

Chicken Enchilada Dip,
page 62

Classic Convenience

ideal slow cooker
6-quart

Collard Greens

Have some cornbread or rolls handy for sopping up the juices. A sprinkling of pepper sauce is the ultimate Southern condiment for these greens.

makes 10 to 12 servings • hands-on time: 5 min. • total time: 9 hr., 5 min.

1 smoked turkey wing (about 1¼ lb.)
2 (14-oz.) cans Italian-seasoned chicken broth
2 (1-lb.) packages chopped fresh collard greens
5 green onions, chopped
1 green bell pepper, seeded and coarsely chopped
¾ tsp. salt
½ tsp. black pepper
Pepper sauce

1. Remove skin and meat from turkey wing, discarding skin and bone. Coarsely chop meat.

2. Combine chopped turkey and next 6 ingredients in a 6-qt. slow cooker.

3. Cover and cook on LOW 9 hours or until greens are tender. Serve with pepper sauce.

Barbecue Baked Beans

This recipe's 12-hour cook time allows you the flexibility to go to work, come home, fire up the grill, and entertain guests—the beans will be done just in time for dinner to be served.

makes 9 servings • hands-on time: 20 min. • total time: 13 hr., 20 min.

1   (20-oz.) package dried Cajun 15-bean soup mix
1   (12-oz.) package diced cooked ham
2   cups chicken broth
1   cup chopped onion
1   (18-oz.) bottle hickory smoke barbecue sauce
¼   cup firmly packed light brown sugar
¼   cup molasses
½   tsp. salt
¼   tsp. ground red pepper

1. Reserve seasoning packet in soup mix for another use. Place beans in a large glass bowl; add water 2 inches above beans. Microwave at HIGH 15 minutes; cover and let stand 1 hour. Drain.

2. Combine beans, ham, broth, and onion in a 5-qt. slow cooker. Combine barbecue sauce and remaining ingredients in a small bowl; stir into bean mixture.

3. Cover and cook on LOW 12 hours or until beans are tender and sauce is slightly thickened.

Note: We tested with Hurst's HamBeens Cajun 15 Bean Soup, Hormel Cure 81 ham.

Peppered Corn on the Cob

makes 5 servings • hands-on time: 13 min. • total time: 4 hr., 13 min.

6 Tbsp. butter, softened
4 garlic cloves, pressed
5 ears fresh corn, husks removed
1 tsp. freshly ground pepper
½ tsp. salt
15 fully cooked bacon slices
½ cup chicken broth
1 jalapeño pepper, minced

1. Combine butter and garlic in a small bowl. Rub garlic butter evenly over ears of corn. Sprinkle evenly with pepper and salt. Wrap each ear of corn with 3 bacon slices, and secure with wooden picks. Place corn in a 5-qt. slow cooker. Add broth and jalapeño.

2. Cover and cook on LOW 3 to 4 hours or until corn is tender. Remove bacon before serving, if desired.

Note: We tested with Eckrich Ready Crisp Bacon.

Make It *Easier*

If you don't want to wrap the bacon around the corn, simply chop the bacon and sprinkle on top of the corn in the cooker.

Hot-and-Spicy Black-eyed Peas

makes 12 cups • hands-on time: 20 min. • total time: 16 hr., 50 min.

1 (16-oz.) package dried black-eyed peas

4 green onions, chopped

1 red bell pepper, chopped

1 jalapeño pepper, diced

1 (3-oz.) package pepperoni slices, diced

1 chicken bouillon cube

½ tsp. salt

¼ tsp. ground red pepper

1 (14½-oz.) can Mexican-style stewed tomatoes

¾ cup uncooked quick white rice

1. Place peas in a large bowl. Cover with 2 cups hot water 2 inches above peas; let stand 8 hours. Drain.

2. Combine peas and next 7 ingredients in a 5-qt. slow cooker.

3. Cover and cook on LOW 8 hours or until beans are tender. Stir in tomatoes and rice. Cover and cook on LOW 30 more minutes or until rice is tender.

Secret Ingredients

Jalapeño pepper and Mexican-style stewed tomatoes add a touch of heat and fresh flavor to the black-eyed peas, a traditional Southern side dish.

ideal slow cooker
7-quart oval

Mexican Spoonbread-Stuffed Poblanos

We used frozen chopped onion to ensure it was tender after cooking. If you use fresh onion, cook it briefly in the microwave, or finely chop it before cooking.

makes 6 servings • hands-on time: 20 min. • total time: 4 hr., 20 min.

6   poblano chile peppers
¾   cup self-rising cornmeal mix
⅔   cup frozen chopped onion, thawed
1   (8-oz.) can cream-style corn
1   cup (4 oz.) shredded Colby Jack
      cheese
1   large egg, lightly beaten
¼   cup milk
2   Tbsp. butter, melted
2   Tbsp. canned chopped green
      chiles
½   tsp. salt
⅛   tsp. hot sauce

1. Lay peppers on sides. Slice off top quarter of peppers lengthwise to create shells. Reserve removed portions of peppers for other uses. Scrape out seeds using a small spoon; discard seeds.

2. Combine cornmeal mix and remaining 9 ingredients in a medium bowl. Spoon cornmeal mixture into pepper shells. Arrange peppers in a 7-qt. oval slow cooker. Cover and cook on HIGH 4 hours.

Cajun Succotash

makes 8 servings • hands-on time: 6 min. • total time: 4 hr., 6 min.

2 cups frozen whole kernel corn

1 (14-oz.) can low-sodium fat-free vegetable broth

1½ tsp. Cajun seasoning

3 garlic cloves, minced

2 (16-oz.) cans red beans, drained and rinsed

1 (28-oz.) can diced tomatoes, undrained

1 (16-oz.) package frozen cut okra

1 large onion, chopped

Hot cooked brown rice

1. Combine all ingredients except rice in a 5-qt. slow cooker. Cover and cook on LOW 4 hours. Serve over hot cooked brown rice.

Secret Ingredient

The long slow-cooking time really coaxes the flavor of the spicy Cajun seasoning into the red beans, adding a nice zest of flavor to the dish.

ideal slow cooker
5-quart

Apple-Pecan Sweet Potatoes

makes 6 servings • hands-on time: 15 min. • total time: 8 hr., 15 min.

4   large sweet potatoes, peeled and cut into 1½-inch cubes

1½   cups peeled and chopped Granny Smith apple (1 large apple)

1   cup chicken broth

½   cup whipping cream

¼   cup firmly packed light brown sugar

2   Tbsp. butter

½   tsp. salt

¾   tsp. ground cinnamon

¾   cup chopped pecans, toasted

1. Combine first 3 ingredients in a 5-quart slow cooker. Cover and cook on LOW 8 hours or until potatoes are tender; drain, discarding broth.

2. Add whipping cream and next 4 ingredients; beat at medium speed with an electric mixer until smooth and blended. Stir in pecans.

How to Pack Brown Sugar

Brown sugar must be packed into the measuring cup to get an accurate measurement. Spoon it into a dry measuring cup that is the size the recipe specifies, and press it with the back of a spoon. Continue to add and pack more sugar until it reaches the rim. Level with the flat side of a knife.

Mexican Macaroni

makes 6 servings • hands-on time: 10 min. • total time: 3 hr., 16 min.

1 (8-oz.) package elbow macaroni, uncooked

1 (10-oz.) can diced tomatoes and green chiles, undrained

1 (10¾-oz.) can cream of mushroom soup, undiluted

1 (8-oz.) container sour cream

1 (4.5-oz.) can chopped green chiles

2 cups (8 oz.) shredded Mexican four-cheese blend

1. Cook macaroni in boiling water for 6 minutes. Stir together macaroni, diced tomatoes, and next 3 ingredients with 1 cup water in a bowl; stir in 1½ cups cheese. Pour mixture into a lightly greased 3-quart slow cooker; top with remaining ½ cup cheese.

2. Cover and cook on LOW 3 hours or until macaroni is done.

Slow-Cooker School

You get a much better texture on the macaroni in this recipe if you cook it just a bit before placing it in the slow cooker.

Texas Stew

makes 12 cups • hands-on time: 10 min. • total time: 4 hr., 10 min.

2 lb. beef tips, cut into 1-inch cubes
1 (14½-oz.) can Mexican-style stewed tomatoes, undrained
1 (10½-oz.) can condensed beef broth
1 (8-oz.) jar mild picante sauce
1 (10-oz.) package frozen whole kernel corn, thawed
3 carrots, cut into ½-inch pieces
1 onion, cut into thin wedges
2 garlic cloves, pressed
½ tsp. ground cumin
½ tsp. salt
¼ cup all-purpose flour

1. Combine first 10 ingredients in a 5-qt. slow cooker.

2. Cover and cook on HIGH 3 to 4 hours or until meat is tender.

3. Stir together ½ cup water and flour. Stir into meat mixture; cover and cook on HIGH 1 more hour or until thickened.

Secret Ingredient

If mild picante sauce is not spicy enough for you then kick it up a notch with hot picante sauce. If you like it really hot, add chopped jalapeño.

Hoppin' John Chowder

Adding boil-in-bag rice at the end keeps it from overcooking.

makes 18 cups • hands-on time: 14 min. • total time: 6 hr., 34 min.

4	(15.8-oz.) cans black-eyed peas, undrained
2	(10-oz.) cans diced tomatoes and green chiles, undrained
1	(14-oz.) can beef broth
1	lb. smoked sausage, sliced
1	cup finely chopped onion
¾	cup chopped green bell pepper
½	tsp. garlic powder
¼	tsp. salt
¼	tsp. black pepper
1	family-size package boil-in-bag rice, uncooked (about 1½ cups uncooked)

1. Combine first 9 ingredients and 1 cup water in a 6-qt. slow cooker.

2. Cover and cook on LOW 6 hours. Cut top off boil-in-bag rice; pour rice into slow cooker, and discard bag. Stir.

3. Cover and cook on HIGH 20 minutes or until rice is tender.

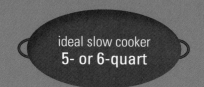
Pot Likker Soup

makes 6 to 8 servings • hands-on time: 10 min. • total time: 6 hr., 10 min.

1   Tbsp. olive oil
2   cups refrigerated prechopped
    onion
½   cup chopped carrot
2   garlic cloves, minced
1   (1-lb.) ham hock
4   (1-lb.) packages fresh collard
    greens, cleaned, trimmed, and
    chopped
½   tsp. salt
½   tsp. freshly ground pepper
¼   tsp. dried crushed red pepper
1   (32-oz.) container chicken broth

1. Heat oil in a large skillet over medium-high heat; add onion and carrot, and sauté 4 minutes or until tender. Add garlic; sauté 1 minute. Place vegetables, 4 cups water, ham hock, and remaining ingredients in a 5- or 6-qt. slow cooker. Cover and cook on HIGH 1 hour. Reduce heat to LOW, and cook 5 hours or until ham falls off the bone. Remove ham hock from slow cooker. Remove ham from bone, discarding bone. Chop ham, and stir into soup.

How to Select Sauté Pans

Use either a skillet (a wide pan with sloped sides) or a sauté pan (a wide pan with straight sides). Both have a large surface area so food is less likely to become overcrowded. Choose a pan with a dense bottom that evenly distributes heat. Non-stick, anodized aluminum, and stainless steel options work well.

Brunswick Stew

Cooking on low heat for a long time makes the meat extremely tender, so it shreds easily. High heat yields a less tender product.

makes 8 servings • hands-on time: 15 min. • total time: 10 hr., 15 min.

3	lb. boneless pork shoulder roast (Boston butt)
2	medium-size new potatoes, peeled and chopped
1	large onion, chopped
1	(28-oz.) can crushed tomatoes
1	(18-oz.) bottle barbecue sauce
1	(14-oz.) can chicken broth
1	(9-oz.) package frozen baby lima beans, thawed
1	(9-oz.) package frozen whole kernel corn, thawed
6	Tbsp. brown sugar
1	tsp. salt

1. Trim roast, and cut into 2-inch pieces. Stir together all ingredients in a 6-qt. slow cooker.

2. Cover and cook on LOW 10 hours or until potatoes are fork-tender. Remove pork with a slotted spoon, and shred with two forks. Return shredded pork to slow cooker, and stir well. Ladle stew into bowls.

Spicy Chicken Chili Verde

Mashing some of the beans at the end of cooking thickens the chili slightly and gives it more body and a creamy texture.

makes 6 servings • hands-on time: 8 min. • total time: 10 hr., 8 min.

1   lb. skinned and boned chicken thighs, cut into 1-inch pieces
1   Tbsp. vegetable oil
1   (8-oz.) container refrigerated prechopped onion
1   Tbsp. jarred minced garlic
2   cups chicken broth
1   cup salsa verde
1   cup frozen whole kernel corn
1   tsp. ground cumin
1   tsp. hot sauce
½   tsp. pepper
1   (15.5-oz.) can cannellini beans, drained
Garnishes: sour cream, chopped tomato, chopped fresh cilantro

1. Cook chicken in hot oil in a medium skillet over medium-high heat 4 minutes or until browned, stirring often. Transfer chicken to a 4-qt. slow cooker, reserving drippings in skillet. Add onion and garlic to drippings; sauté until vegetables are tender. Add broth, stirring to loosen particles from bottom of skillet. Add broth mixture to chicken in slow cooker. Stir in salsa and next 4 ingredients. Cover and cook on LOW 10 hours.

2. Add beans. Mash beans in soup with a potato masher or the back of a spoon to desired consistency. Garnish, if desired.

ideal slow cooker
5-quart

Grillades and Cheese Grits

makes 6 servings • hands-on time: 15 min. • total time: 6 hr., 30 min.

2 lb. top round steak (about ½ inch thick)

1 tsp. salt, divided

¼ tsp. pepper

¼ cup all-purpose flour, divided

2 Tbsp. vegetable oil

2 (8-oz.) containers refrigerated prechopped celery, onion, and bell pepper mix

3 garlic cloves, minced

1 (14-oz.) can beef broth

1 tsp. dried Italian seasoning

½ tsp. ground red pepper

2 (14.5-oz.) cans diced tomatoes with basil, garlic, and oregano

2 cups uncooked quick-cooking grits

2 cups (8 oz.) Gruyère cheese, shredded

Garnish: chopped fresh parsley

1. Sprinkle steak with ½ tsp. salt and pepper. Set aside 1 Tbsp. flour. Cut steak into 2-inch pieces; dredge in remaining flour.

2. Heat oil in a large nonstick skillet over medium-high heat; add steak, and cook 3 minutes on each side or until browned. Transfer to a 5-qt. slow cooker. Add celery mix and garlic to skillet; sauté 3 minutes. Add beef broth, stirring to loosen particles from bottom of skillet. Stir in Italian seasoning and red pepper. Pour mixture over steak. Drain 1 can tomatoes. Add drained tomatoes and remaining can tomatoes to steak mixture. Cover and cook on LOW 6 hours or until steak is very tender.

3. Increase heat to HIGH. Stir together reserved flour and 2 Tbsp. water until smooth; gently stir into steak mixture. Cover and cook 15 minutes or until mixture is slightly thickened.

4. Meanwhile, bring 8 cups water and remaining ½ tsp. salt to a boil in a 4-qt. saucepan; gradually whisk in grits. Reduce heat, and simmer, whisking often, 5 minutes or until thickened; stir in cheese. Serve grillades over grits. Garnish, if desired.

How to Sauté Meat

Browning meat before slow cooking enhances the flavor and appearance of the meat. When sautéing bite-size pieces of meat, stir frequently to promote even browning and cooking. Portion-size cuts of meat should be turned only once so they have enough time to form a nice crust. This keeps the meat from sticking to the pan.

Beef Brisket Soft Tacos

Select a brisket that is uniform in thickness to make shredding the meat easier.

makes 6 to 8 servings • hands-on time: 15 min. • total time: 6 hr., 15 min.

2   medium onions, thinly sliced
2   celery ribs, thinly sliced
2   garlic cloves, pressed
1   (2-lb.) beef brisket
2   tsp. salt
1½ tsp. ground chipotle powder
1   cup coarsely chopped fresh
     cilantro
10   (8-inch) flour tortillas
Toppings: shredded Mexican cheese
     blend, sour cream, salsa, chopped
     fresh cilantro
Lime wedges

1. Place first 3 ingredients in a 6-qt. slow cooker.

2. Trim fat from brisket; cut into 3-inch pieces. Rub brisket pieces with salt and chipotle powder, and place on top of vegetables in slow cooker. Top with cilantro.

3. Cover and cook on HIGH 6 hours or until brisket pieces shred easily with a fork.

4. Remove brisket from slow cooker, and cool slightly. Using 2 forks, shred meat into bite-size pieces. Return mixture to slow cooker. Serve in flour tortillas with desired toppings and lime wedges.

"Cowboy" Pot Roast

"Cowboy" is often used for recipes that have the "flavors of Texas," such as the tomatoes with green chiles, chili powder, pinto/black beans, and pickled jalapeños used here.

makes 6 servings • hands-on time: 15 min. • total time: 8 hr., 35 min.

1½ tsp. salt, divided
1½ tsp. pepper, divided
1   (14.5-oz.) can petite-cut diced tomatoes, drained
1   (10-oz.) can diced tomatoes and green chiles, undrained
1   onion, cut into 8 wedges
1   Tbsp. chili powder
1   (2½- to 3-lb.) eye-of-round roast, trimmed
2   Tbsp. vegetable oil
2   (16-oz.) cans pinto beans, drained
1   (15-oz.) can black beans, drained
Pickled jalapeño pepper slices (optional)

1. Combine 1 tsp. salt, 1 tsp. pepper, and next 4 ingredients in a medium bowl. Sprinkle roast with remaining ½ tsp. salt and ½ tsp. pepper. Brown roast on all sides in hot oil in a large Dutch oven over medium-high heat. Transfer roast to a 5-qt. slow cooker. Pour tomato mixture over roast. Cover and cook on LOW 8 to 10 hours or until very tender.

2. Remove roast from slow cooker; cut into large chunks. Keep warm.

3. Skim fat from juices in slow cooker. Mash 1½ cans (about 2¾ cups) pinto beans; add to slow cooker, and stir until combined. Stir in black beans and remaining ½ can pinto beans. Return roast pieces to slow cooker; cover and cook on HIGH 20 minutes. Top each serving with jalapeño pepper slices, if desired.

ideal slow cooker
5- or 6-quart oval

Home-style Meatloaf

Use a meat thermometer to test the loaf's doneness (160° for ground beef, pork, or veal; 165° for ground poultry).

makes 8 servings • hands-on time: 11 min. • total time: 4 hr., 36 min.

2	Tbsp. butter
1	(8-oz.) container refrigerated prechopped celery, onion, and bell pepper mix
2	garlic cloves, minced
2	lb. ground round
¾	cup uncooked quick-cooking oats
1	cup ketchup, divided
¾	tsp. salt
½	tsp. freshly ground pepper
2	large eggs, lightly beaten
2	Tbsp. brown sugar
1	Tbsp. yellow mustard

1. Melt butter in a large skillet over medium-high heat. Add celery mixture and garlic; sauté 3 minutes or until tender. Combine vegetable mixture, ground round, oats, ½ cup ketchup, salt, pepper, and eggs in a large bowl.

2. Shape mixture into a 9- x 4-inch loaf; place in a lightly greased 5- or 6-qt. oval slow cooker.

3. Cover and cook on HIGH 1 hour. Reduce heat to LOW, and cook 3 hours. Remove slow cooker insert, and carefully pour off excess fat. Return insert to cooker.

4. Stir together remaining ½ cup ketchup, brown sugar, and mustard. Spread over meatloaf. Cover and cook on LOW 15 minutes or until no longer pink in center. Remove meatloaf from slow cooker, and let stand 10 minutes before serving.

Cajun Dirty Rice

makes 8 servings • hands-on time: 10 min. • total time: 2 hr., 10 min.

1   lb. lean ground beef
1   lb. ground pork sausage
2   tsp. Cajun seasoning
2   (8-oz.) containers refrigerated prechopped celery, onion, and bell pepper mix
2   cups uncooked converted long-grain rice
¼   tsp. ground red pepper
1   (10-oz.) can diced tomatoes with green chiles, undrained
1   cup chicken broth

1. Brown first 3 ingredients in a large skillet over medium-high heat, stirring often, 8 minutes or until meat crumbles and is no longer pink. Transfer mixture to a 5-qt. slow cooker using a slotted spoon.

2. Stir in celery mix and remaining ingredients. Cover and cook on LOW 2 hours or until liquid is absorbed and rice is tender.

Slow-Cooker School

Rice can be prepared successfully in the slow cooker if you use the right type. Use converted rice because its firmer grain can stand up to the longer cooking time without becoming gummy.

Spaghetti Casserole

makes 6 to 8 servings • hands-on time: 26 min. • total time: 4 hr., 36 min.

1½ lb. ground round
1   medium onion, chopped
1   (24-oz.) jar tomato and basil
     pasta sauce
¼   cup butter
¼   cup all-purpose flour
1   (12-oz.) can evaporated milk
½   cup grated Parmesan cheese
¼   tsp. pepper
8   oz. uncooked spaghetti, broken
     into pieces
3   cups (12 oz.) shredded sharp
     Cheddar cheese
Grated Parmesan cheese

1. Cook ground round and onion in a large skillet, stirring until beef crumbles and is no longer pink; drain meat, and return to skillet. Stir pasta sauce into beef mixture.

2. Melt butter in a saucepan over medium-low heat; whisk in flour until smooth. Cook 1 minute, whisking constantly. Gradually whisk in milk; cook over medium heat, whisking constantly, 8 minutes or until mixture is thickened and bubbly. Remove from heat, and stir in ½ cup Parmesan cheese and pepper.

3. Spoon one-third of meat mixture into a lightly greased 5-qt. slow cooker. Spread half of broken spaghetti over meat; pour half of white sauce over noodles, and sprinkle with 1 cup Cheddar cheese. Repeat layers once. Spread remaining meat mixture over cheese. Top with remaining 1 cup Cheddar cheese. Cover and cook on LOW 4 hours. Let stand 10 minutes before serving. Serve with Parmesan cheese.

Thai-Style Ribs

makes 2 to 4 servings • hands-on time: 10 min. • total time: 14 hr., 10 min.

3½ lb. pork baby back ribs, racks cut in half

1 (11.5-oz.) can frozen orange-pineapple-apple juice concentrate, thawed and undiluted

¾ cup soy sauce

¼ cup creamy peanut butter

¼ cup minced fresh cilantro

2 Tbsp. minced fresh ginger

1 garlic clove, pressed

2 tsp. sugar

Garnish: fresh cilantro sprigs

1. Place ribs in a large shallow dish or zip-top freezer bag.

2. Combine juice concentrate and next 6 ingredients in a small bowl stirring with a wire whisk. Reserve ¾ cup mixture in refrigerator for dipping. Pour remaining mixture over ribs; cover or seal, and chill 8 hours, turning occasionally.

3. Remove ribs from marinade, discarding marinade. Place 1 rack of ribs in bottom of a 6-qt. slow cooker; stand remaining rib racks on their sides around edges of slow cooker. Cover and cook on HIGH 1 hour. Reduce heat to LOW, and cook 5 hours.

4. Microwave reserved ¾ cup sauce in a 1-cup glass measuring cup at HIGH 1 to 1½ minutes or until thoroughly heated, stirring once. Serve with ribs. Garnish, if desired.

Orange-Molasses BBQ Ribs

Browning the ribs in the oven renders water and excess fat, making the sauce thicker.

makes 6 servings • hands-on time: 20 min. • total time: 8 hr., 30 min.

Cooking spray
2 slabs pork baby back ribs (about 5 lb.), cut in half
1 cup barbecue sauce
¼ cup molasses
¼ cup frozen orange juice concentrate, thawed
2 tsp. hot sauce
1 tsp. jarred minced garlic
¼ tsp. salt
Garnish: orange slices

1. Preheat broiler with oven rack 5½ inches from heat. Coat the rack of a broiler pan and broiler pan with cooking spray. Place ribs on rack in broiler pan. Broil 10 minutes.

2. Meanwhile, stir together barbecue sauce and next 5 ingredients in a medium bowl.

3. Arrange ribs in a 6-qt. oval slow cooker. Pour sauce over ribs.

4. Cover and cook on LOW 8 hours. Transfer ribs to a serving platter. Skim fat from juices in slow cooker. Pour juices into a 2-qt. sauce-pan. Cook over medium-high heat 10 minutes or until reduced to 1½ cups, stirring occasionally. Serve sauce with ribs. Garnish, if desired.

Spiced Apple Pork Chops

makes 4 servings • hands-on time: 12 min. • total time: 6 hr., 12 min.

4 (1¼-inch-thick) pork chops (about 3 lb.)
1 tsp. salt, divided
½ tsp. pepper
1 (8-oz.) container refrigerated prechopped onion (about 1¾ cups)
½ cup raisins
2 (5-oz.) packages dried apples
½ cup firmly packed brown sugar
1 Tbsp. ground cinnamon
½ tsp. ground cloves
½ tsp. ground ginger

1. Sprinkle pork with ½ tsp. salt and pepper. Heat a large nonstick skillet over medium-high heat. Add pork to pan; cook 3 minutes on each side or until browned. Transfer pork to a lightly greased 5-qt. slow cooker, reserving drippings in pan.

2. Sauté onion in drippings 3 minutes or until tender. Add onion, remaining ½ tsp. salt, 2 cups water, raisins, and remaining 5 ingredients to pork in slow cooker. Cover and cook on LOW 6 hours.

Slow-Cooker School

The thickness of the pork chops is essential in this recipe. It ensures that this lean cut of pork stays tender and juicy throughout the long cook time.

Pimiento Cheese Grits with Ham

makes 6 servings • hands-on time: 4 min. • total time: 6 hr., 4 min.

4½ cups low-sodium fat-free chicken broth
3   Tbsp. butter, melted
1½ cups uncooked stone-ground yellow grits
½   tsp. freshly ground pepper
1   lb. fully cooked smoked ham, cut into 1-inch cubes
3   (2-oz.) jars diced pimiento, drained
1   cup (4 oz.) shredded Cheddar cheese
½   cup (2 oz.) shredded Swiss cheese
½   cup heavy cream

1. Whisk together broth and butter in a lightly greased 4-qt. slow cooker; gradually whisk in grits and pepper. Stir in ham and pimiento. Cover and cook on LOW 6 hours, stirring after 3 hours.

2. Stir in cheeses and cream. Serve immediately.

Cheesy Ham and Noodles

This family-friendly pasta dish is adaptable: Use your favorite type of frozen vegetables, and substitute whipping cream and Gruyère cheese for the half-and-half and Swiss cheese.

makes 6 servings • hands-on time: 9 min. • total time: 3 hr., 9 min.

12 oz. uncooked linguine

3 cups half-and-half

2 cups (8 oz.) shredded Swiss cheese

1 cup frozen peas

1 Tbsp. Dijon mustard

1 (12-oz.) lean ham steak, chopped

1 (10-oz.) package refrigerated Alfredo sauce

1. Cook linguine 5 minutes in boiling water in a 4-qt. saucepan; drain. Transfer linguine to a lightly greased 4-qt. slow cooker. Add half-and-half, 1 cup cheese, and next 4 ingredients, stirring gently to blend. Sprinkle with remaining 1 cup cheese. Cover and cook on LOW 3 hours or until linguine is tender.

ideal slow cooker
5-quart

Sausage, Red Beans, and Rice

makes 8 servings • hands-on time: 14 min. • total time: 16 hr., 14 min.

1 (16-oz.) package dried red beans
1 lb. smoked sausage, sliced
1 cup chopped onion
¾ cup chopped parsley
1 tsp. salt
½ tsp. dried oregano
½ tsp. dried thyme
⅛ tsp. ground red pepper
3 garlic cloves, minced
Hot cooked rice
Hot sauce
Chopped green onions

1. Rinse and sort beans according to package directions. Cover with water 2 inches above beans; let soak 8 hours. Drain and place in a 5-qt. slow cooker.

2. Sauté sausage and onion in a large skillet over medium-high heat 5 minutes or until sausage is browned and onion is tender.

3. Stir sausage mixture, 5 cups water, parsley, and next 5 ingredients into beans. Cover and cook on LOW 8 hours. Mash beans with a potato masher or the back of a spoon to desired consistency. Serve with rice and hot sauce; sprinkle with green onions.

How to Store Fresh Herbs

When storing a bunch of fresh herbs, wrap the stems in a damp paper towel, and store them in a zip-top plastic bag. Wash herbs just before using; pat them dry with a paper towel.

Louisiana-Style Smothered Pork Chops

makes 4 servings • hands-on time: 15 min. • total time: 6 hr., 25 min.

4   oz. smoked sausage, chopped
3   Tbsp. all-purpose flour
1   tsp. salt
½   tsp. pepper
4   (1¼-inch-thick) bone-in center-cut
     pork chops
3   Tbsp. vegetable oil
1   (16-oz.) package frozen gumbo
     vegetable mix
1   (14-oz.) can chicken broth
½   tsp. dried thyme
1   Tbsp. cornstarch
Hot cooked rice
4   green onions, sliced
Hot sauce (optional)

1. Sauté sausage in a large skillet over medium-high heat until browned. Drain sausage, reserving drippings in pan.

2. Combine flour, salt, and pepper in a large zip-top plastic freezer bag; add pork chops. Seal bag, and shake to coat.

3. Add oil to drippings in skillet. Cook pork chops in hot oil over medium-high heat 3 minutes on each side or until browned. Transfer pork chops to a 5- or 6-qt. slow cooker. Layer vegetables and sausage over pork chops; add broth and thyme. Cover and cook on LOW 6 hours.

4. Remove pork chops from slow cooker; cover and keep warm. Increase temperature to HIGH. Combine cornstarch and 2 Tbsp. water, stirring until smooth. Stir cornstarch mixture into vegetables in slow cooker. Cook, uncovered, 10 minutes or until thickened.

5. Spoon rice onto serving plates; top with pork chops. Spoon vegetables and sauce over pork chops. Sprinkle vegetables with green onions, and serve with hot sauce, if desired.

Chicken Enchilada Dip

makes 8 servings • hands-on time: 10 min. • total time: 4 hr., 10 min. • pictured on page 22

2   (10-oz.) cans mild green chile
       enchilada sauce, divided

10   (6-inch) corn tortillas, torn into
       3-inch pieces, divided

4   cups pulled cooked chicken
       breasts

1½   cups sour cream

1   (12-oz.) package shredded
       Colby-Jack cheese blend, divided

1   (10¾-oz.) can cream of mushroom
       soup

8   cups shredded iceberg lettuce

1   (15-oz.) can black beans, drained
       and rinsed

3   tomatoes, diced

1. Spoon ½ cup enchilada sauce over bottom of a greased 4-qt. slow cooker. Add enough tortilla pieces to cover sauce.

2. Stir together chicken, sour cream, 2 cups cheese, and soup. Spread 2 cups chicken mixture over tortilla pieces. Top with tortilla pieces to cover. Drizzle with ½ cup enchilada sauce. Repeat layers twice, ending with tortilla pieces and remaining enchilada sauce. Sprinkle with remaining 1 cup cheese.

3. Cover and cook on LOW 4 hours. Place lettuce on plates; top with chicken dip, beans, and tomatoes. Serve hot.

Secret Ingredient

The corn tortillas cook into this dish and thicken it—you won't see them after they're cooked, but you will still taste their authentic Mexican flavor.

Poppy-Seed Chicken

Don't be tempted to sprinkle on the cracker-crumb mixture while the chicken is in the cooker—condensation will make them soggy.

makes 6 servings • hands-on time: 5 min. • total time: 4 hr., 5 min.

6   skinned and boned chicken breasts
2   (10¾-oz.) cans cream of chicken soup
1   cup milk
1   Tbsp. poppy seeds
36   round buttery crackers, crushed
¼   cup butter, melted

1. Place chicken in a lightly greased 6-qt. oval slow cooker. Whisk together soup, milk, and poppy seeds in a medium bowl; pour over chicken. Cover and cook on HIGH 1 hour.

2. Reduce heat to LOW, and cook 3 hours.

3. Combine cracker crumbs and butter, stirring until crumbs are moistened. Sprinkle over chicken just before serving.

Chicken and Dumplings

makes 8 servings • hands-on time: 23 min. • total time: 8 hr., 38 min.

5   large carrots, cut into 2-inch pieces

3   small Yukon gold potatoes, cut into chunks

6   skinned and boned chicken breasts

1   tsp. salt

1   tsp. freshly ground pepper

Cooking spray

1   cup chicken broth or water

2   (10¾-oz.) cans cream of chicken soup

Freshly ground pepper

1   cup frozen peas

2   hard-cooked eggs, chopped

2   cups all-purpose baking mix

⅔   cup half-and-half or milk

2   Tbsp. chopped fresh herbs, such as flat-leaf parsley, thyme, and rosemary

Garnishes: chopped fresh herbs, freshly ground pepper

1. Place carrot and potato in a lightly greased 6-qt. slow cooker.

2. Sprinkle chicken with 1 tsp. each of salt and pepper. Heat a large nonstick skillet over medium-high heat. Coat with cooking spray. Sauté chicken, in 2 batches, 2 minutes on each side or until browned. Place chicken over vegetables in slow cooker. Stir together broth and soup; pour over chicken. Sprinkle with freshly ground pepper.

3. Cover and cook on LOW 7 hours. Add peas and eggs, stirring gently to break up chicken into bite-size pieces.

4. Combine baking mix, half-and-half, and herbs; stir with a fork until blended. Drop 8 spoonfuls onto chicken mixture. Cover and cook on HIGH 1 hour and 15 minutes or until dumplings are done. Garnish, if desired.

Buffalo Chicken Sandwiches

makes 6 servings • hands-on time: 7 min. • total time: 3 hr., 9 min.

4   skinned and boned chicken
    breasts
¼   tsp. salt
⅛   tsp. freshly ground pepper
1   Tbsp. olive oil
1   (14-oz.) bottle Buffalo wing sauce,
    divided
2   small celery ribs
¾   cup matchstick carrots
1   Tbsp. thinly sliced red onion
⅓   cup refrigerated blue cheese
    dressing
6   bakery-style buns or kaiser rolls,
    lightly toasted

1. Sprinkle chicken with salt and ground pepper. Heat oil in a large nonstick skillet over medium-high heat. Add chicken; cook 2 minutes on each side or until lightly browned. Transfer chicken to a 4-qt. slow cooker. Reserve 2 Tbsp. wing sauce. Pour remaining wing sauce over chicken. Cover and cook on LOW 3 hours or until chicken is done.

2. Meanwhile, thinly slice celery crosswise to measure ¾ cup. Combine reserved 2 Tbsp. wing sauce, celery, carrot, and next 2 ingredients; toss to coat.

3. Transfer chicken to a bowl and shred with 2 forks; toss with ½ cup cooking liquid from slow cooker. Serve shredded chicken on buns; top with carrot slaw.

King Ranch Chicken

makes 6 servings • hands-on time: 10 min. • total time: 4 hr., 10 min.

4   cups chopped cooked chicken

1   large onion, chopped

1   large green bell pepper, chopped

1   (10¾-oz.) can cream of chicken soup

1   (10¾-oz.) can cream of mushroom soup

1   (10-oz.) can diced tomatoes and green chiles

1   garlic clove, minced

1   tsp. chili powder

12   (6-inch) fajita-size corn tortillas

2   cups (8 oz.) shredded sharp Cheddar cheese

1. Stir together first 8 ingredients. Tear tortillas into 1-inch pieces; layer one-third of tortilla pieces in a lightly greased 6-qt. slow cooker. Top with one-third of chicken mixture and ⅔ cup cheese. Repeat layers twice.

2. Cover and cook on LOW 3½ hours or until bubbly and edges are golden brown. Uncover and cook on LOW 30 minutes.

Make It *Easier*

Purchase a rotisserie chicken at the deli of the grocery store. To save even more time, ask the deli to chop the chicken for you.

Peach-Ginger Wings

makes 4 servings • hands-on time: 15 min. • total time: 4 hr., 15 min.

4 lb. halved chicken wings (about 32 wing pieces)
1 cup peach preserves
½ cup soy sauce
2 Tbsp. grated fresh ginger
1 Tbsp. frozen limeade concentrate, thawed
1 Tbsp. jarred minced garlic
¼ tsp. hot sauce

1. Preheat broiler. Place wings on a lightly greased rack in a lightly greased broiler pan. Broil 3 inches from heat 14 minutes or until browned. Transfer wings to a lightly greased 5-qt. slow cooker.

2. While wings broil, stir together preserves and remaining ingredients in a small bowl. Pour peach mixture over wings. Cover and cook on LOW 4 hours.

How to Prepare Fresh Ginger

1. Use a vegetable peeler to remove the skin and reveal the yellowish flesh.
2. For chopped or minced ginger, place a peeled piece on a cutting board. Cut with the grain into thin strips; stack the slices. Cut across the pile into small pieces.
3. For grated ginger, rub a peeled piece of ginger across a fine grater, such as a Microplane.

Shrimp Creole

makes 6 to 8 servings • hands-on time: 8 min. • total time: 2 hr., 8 min.

4   bacon slices
½   cup chopped red bell pepper
1   (8-oz.) container refrigerated
     prechopped celery, onion, and
     bell pepper mix
3   garlic cloves, minced
2   Tbsp. chopped fresh parsley
1   tsp. Cajun seasoning
1   bay leaf
¼   tsp. salt
¼   tsp. freshly ground pepper
2   (14.5-oz.) cans stewed tomatoes
1½   lb. peeled and deveined large
     raw shrimp
Hot cooked rice
Garnish: chopped fresh parsley

1. Cook bacon in a skillet over medium-high heat 4 to 5 minutes or until crisp; remove bacon, and drain on paper towels, reserving drippings in skillet. Crumble bacon. Add red bell pepper and celery mixture to skillet; sauté 3 to 4 minutes or until tender. Add garlic; sauté 1 minute. Combine vegetable mixture, crumbled bacon, parsley, and next 5 ingredients in a lightly greased 4- or 5-qt. slow cooker. Cover and cook on HIGH 1 hour.

2. Stir in shrimp. Cover and cook 45 minutes to 1 hour or until shrimp turn pink. Discard bay leaf. Serve over rice. Garnish, if desired.

Slow-Cooker School

Because shrimp cook so quickly in the slow cooker, you'll want to add them toward the end. Cook them just until they turn pink and opaque.

ideal slow cooker
3-quart

White Chocolate-Coconut Fondue

makes 5½ cups • hands-on time: 11 min. • total time: 1 hr., 11 min.

1 (14-oz.) can sweetened condensed milk
½ cup coconut milk
2 Tbsp. light rum
6 (4-oz.) packages white chocolate baking bars, broken into large pieces
1 (8.8-oz.) container mascarpone cheese, softened
1 cup sweetened flaked coconut, toasted
½ tsp. coconut extract
Cookies, pretzels, strawberries

1. Combine first 3 ingredients in a 3-qt. slow cooker. Stir in chocolate and cheese.

2. Cover and cook on LOW 1 hour. Stir until melted and smooth. Stir in toasted coconut and coconut extract. Keep warm until ready to serve.

Rocky Road Chocolate Cake

makes 8 to 10 servings • hands-on time: 21 min. • total time: 4 hr., 6 min.

1 (18.25-oz.) package German chocolate cake mix

1 (3.9-oz.) package chocolate instant pudding mix

3 large eggs, lightly beaten

1 cup sour cream

⅓ cup butter, melted

1 tsp. vanilla extract

3¼ cups milk, divided

1 (3.4-oz.) package chocolate cook-and-serve pudding mix

½ cup chopped pecans

1½ cups miniature marshmallows

1 cup semisweet chocolate morsels

Vanilla ice cream (optional)

1. Beat cake mix, next 5 ingredients, and 1¼ cups milk at medium speed with an electric mixer 2 minutes, stopping to scrape down sides as needed. Pour batter into a lightly greased 4-qt. slow cooker.

2. Cook remaining 2 cups milk in a heavy nonaluminum saucepan over medium heat, stirring often, 3 to 5 minutes or just until bubbles appear (do not boil); remove from heat.

3. Sprinkle cook-and-serve pudding mix over batter. Slowly pour hot milk over pudding. Cover and cook on LOW 3½ hours.

4. Meanwhile, heat pecans in a small nonstick skillet over medium-low heat, stirring often, 3 to 5 minutes or until lightly toasted and fragrant.

5. Turn off slow cooker. Sprinkle cake with pecans, marshmallows, and chocolate morsels. Let stand 15 minutes or until marshmallows are slightly melted. Spoon into dessert dishes, and serve with ice cream, if desired.

Triple Chocolate-Covered Peanut Clusters

makes 5 pounds or about 60 clusters • hands-on time: 15 min. • total time: 2 hr., 15 min.

1   (16-oz.) jar dry-roasted peanuts

1   (16-oz.) jar unsalted dry-roasted peanuts

18   (2-oz.) chocolate candy coating squares, cut in half

2   cups (12-oz. package) semisweet chocolate morsels

1   (4-oz.) package German chocolate baking squares, broken into pieces

1   (9.75-oz.) can salted whole cashews

1   tsp. vanilla extract

1. Combine first 5 ingredients in a 3½- or 4-qt. slow cooker.

2. Cover and cook on LOW 2 hours or until melted. Stir chocolate mixture. Add cashews and vanilla, stirring well to coat cashews.

3. Drop nut mixture by heaping tablespoonfuls onto wax paper. Let stand until firm. Store in an airtight container.

Make It *Easier*

Make these ahead for your next party or for gift-giving. Clusters may be frozen up to 1 month.

Cinnamon-Raisin Bread Pudding

To quickly make 1-inch bread cubes, stack bread slices and cut vertically into thirds; then cut crosswise into thirds.

makes 8 servings • hands-on time: 13 min. • total time: 4 hr., 13 min.

3   large eggs, beaten
½   cup sugar
1   tsp. ground cinnamon
¼   tsp. ground nutmeg
1   cup milk
1   cup whipping cream
1   tsp. vanilla extract
2   tsp. butter or margarine, melted
1   (1-lb.) cinnamon-raisin bread loaf, cut into 1-inch cubes
½   cup chopped pecans, toasted
Whipped cream (optional)

1. Whisk together first 4 ingredients in a large bowl; stir in milk, whipping cream, vanilla, and butter. Add bread cubes and pecans, stirring gently just until bread is moistened. Cover and chill 1 hour.

2. Pour bread mixture into a lightly greased 2½-quart soufflé dish; cover with aluminum foil. Pour 1 cup water into a 6-qt. round slow cooker; place a wire rack to fit cooker on bottom. Set soufflé dish on rack.

3. Cover and cook on HIGH 3 hours or until a sharp knife inserted into the center comes out clean. Cool slightly before serving. Serve warm with whipped cream, if desired.

Peaches 'n' Cream Tapioca

makes 8 servings • hands-on time: 6 min. • total time: 4 hr., 6 min.

4 cups fresh or frozen peach slices (about 2 lb.)

3 Tbsp. uncooked quick-cooking tapioca

¾ cup firmly packed brown sugar

⅛ tsp. salt

⅛ tsp. ground nutmeg

1 cup heavy whipping cream

½ cup peach nectar

2 cups granola

1. Stir together first 7 ingredients in a 3½-qt. slow cooker.

2. Cover and cook on LOW 4 hours. Stir well; spoon into dessert dishes, and top with granola.

Barbecued Shrimp, page 123

Company's Coming

Queso Blanco

makes 6½ cups • hands-on time: 22 min. • total time: 2 hr., 22 min.

1   small onion, diced

3   garlic cloves, minced

1   (14½-oz.) can petite diced
     tomatoes, drained

1   cup milk

¾   cup pickled jalapeño slices,
     minced

1   Tbsp. juice from jalapeño slices

1   (4½-oz.) can chopped green
     chiles, undrained

1   tsp. ground cumin

½   tsp. dried oregano

½   tsp. coarsely ground pepper

2   lb. deli white American cheese,
     sliced

Pickled jalapeño slices (optional)

Tortilla chips

1. Place onion in a medium-size microwave-safe bowl; cover loosely with heavy-duty plastic wrap. Microwave at HIGH 2 minutes. Stir in garlic and next 8 ingredients.

2. Roughly tear cheese slices; place in a 4-qt. slow cooker. Pour onion mixture over cheese.

3. Cover and cook on LOW 2 hours. Stir gently to blend ingredients. Top with pickled jalapeño slices, if desired. Serve with tortilla chips.

Make It *Easier*

Buy white American cheese by the pound at the deli counter to make this addictive dip. Have the cheese sliced at the deli so you can forgo shredding it; then just roughly tear the slices and place them in the slow cooker. This queso dip freezes well. Spoon into serving-size freezer containers, and freeze up to 1 month. Thaw overnight in refrigerator. Reheat in microwave at MEDIUM.

Baked Pimiento Cheese Dip

The addition of cornstarch to classic pimiento cheese helps keep the oil from separating when the dip is heated. You may want to give it a quick stir before serving.

makes 5 cups • hands-on time: 17 min. • total time: 3 hr., 17 min.

1 (10-oz.) block sharp Cheddar cheese, shredded

1 (10-oz.) block extra-sharp Cheddar cheese, shredded

1 Tbsp. cornstarch

8 bacon slices, cooked and crumbled

½ small onion, finely grated

1 cup mayonnaise

2 (4-oz.) jars diced pimiento, drained

2 tsp. Worcestershire sauce

¼ tsp. pepper

Crackers

1. Toss together cheeses and cornstarch in a medium bowl. Add half of bacon and next 5 ingredients; stir well to blend. Spoon mixture into a lightly greased 3-qt. slow cooker. Sprinkle with remaining bacon.

2. Cover and cook on LOW 2 to 3 hours or until melted and bubbly. Serve warm with crackers.

Note: We tested with Cracker Barrel Sharp and Extra Sharp Cheddar cheeses.

ideal slow cooker
2- or 3-quart

Reuben Spread

makes 3½ cups • hands-on time: 10 min. • total time: 3 hr., 10 min.

½ lb. sliced deli corned beef, coarsely chopped

1 cup sauerkraut, drained, rinsed, and chopped

1 tsp. cider vinegar

¼ tsp. caraway seeds

¼ tsp. pepper

1 (8-oz.) package cream cheese, softened

½ cup Thousand Island dressing

2 cups shredded Swiss cheese

Rye Melba rounds or pretzel rods

1. Stir together first 7 ingredients and 1 cup Swiss cheese; spoon into a lightly greased 2- or 3-qt. slow cooker. Top with remaining 1 cup cheese.

2. Cover and cook on LOW 2 to 3 hours. Serve with rye Melba rounds or pretzel rods.

How to Snip Sauerkraut

Put the drained and rinsed sauerkraut into a small bowl, and use kitchen shears to snip it into more manageable pieces for this dip.

Artichoke and Crabmeat Dip

makes 6 cups • hands-on time: 11 min. • total time: 2 hr., 41 min.

12 oz. fresh lump crabmeat, drained and picked

2 (14-oz.) cans quartered artichoke hearts, drained and chopped

4 garlic cloves, minced

¼ cup lemon juice

4 tsp. hot sauce

½ cup shredded Parmesan cheese

2 (8-oz.) packages cream cheese, softened

¼ tsp. white pepper

1 cup mini bagel chips, coarsely crushed

Bagel chips or pita chips

1. Combine first 8 ingredients. Spoon into a lightly greased 3-qt. slow cooker.

2. Cover and cook on LOW 2½ hours. Stir until cheeses are smooth; sprinkle with crushed bagel chips. Serve with bagel chips or pita chips.

Slow-Cooker School

Don't be afraid to use lump crabmeat in the slow cooker. It's far superior to pasteurized canned crab, and we guarantee this recipe is a winner.

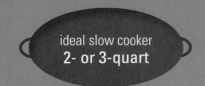
Buffalo Chicken-Cheese Dip

Enjoy the taste of hot wings—without getting your fingers messy. Warm cheese dip with the flavors of buffalo wings makes for an ideal tailgating treat. Bring lots of celery sticks, and watch this dip disappear!

makes 5½ cups • hands-on time: 5 min. • total time: 3 hr., 5 min.

1	Tbsp. vegetable oil
1	onion, chopped
3	cups shredded cooked chicken
¾	to 1 cup hot sauce
1	(8-oz.) package cream cheese, softened
2	cups (8 oz.) shredded Cheddar cheese, divided
Celery sticks	

1. Heat oil in a nonstick skillet over medium-high heat. Add onion, and cook 4 minutes or until onion is tender.

2. Combine onion, chicken, hot sauce, cream cheese, and 1 cup Cheddar cheese in a 2- or 3-qt. slow cooker.

3. Cover and cook on LOW 2½ hours. Remove lid; sprinkle with remaining 1 cup Cheddar cheese. Cover and cook on LOW 30 more minutes or until cheese melts. Serve with celery sticks.

Note: We tested with Frank's RedHot Original Cayenne Pepper Sauce.

Toasted Herbed Rice

makes 6 servings • hands-on time: 7 min. • total time: 2 hr., 7 min.

3   Tbsp. butter

1¾   cups uncooked converted long-grain rice

2   (14-oz.) cans chicken broth

¼   tsp. salt

6   green onions, chopped

1   tsp. dried basil

⅓   cup pine nuts, toasted

Garnish: fresh basil sprig

1. Melt butter in a large skillet over medium-high heat; add rice, and sauté 4 minutes or until golden brown. Combine sautéed rice, broth, and next 3 ingredients in a 4-qt. slow cooker.

2. Cover and cook on HIGH 2 hours or until liquid is absorbed and rice is tender. Stir in pine nuts. Garnish, if desired.

Cornbread Dressing

makes 12 to 16 servings • hands-on time: 20 min. • total time: 6 hr., 20 min.

5 cups crumbled cornbread

1 (14-oz.) package herb stuffing

2 (10¾-oz.) cans cream of chicken soup

2 (14-oz.) cans chicken broth

1 large sweet onion, diced

1 cup diced celery

4 large eggs, lightly beaten

1 Tbsp. rubbed sage

½ tsp. pepper

2 Tbsp. butter, cut up

Garnish: fresh sage leaves

1. Combine first 9 ingredients in a large bowl.

2. Pour cornbread mixture into a lightly greased 6-qt. slow cooker. Dot with butter.

3. Cover and cook on LOW 4 to 6 hours or until set and thoroughly cooked. Garnish, if desired.

Note: Two (6-oz.) packages of Martha White Buttermilk Cornbread & Muffin Mix, prepared according to package directions, yields 5 cups cornbread crumbs. We tested with Pepperidge Farm Herb Seasoned Stuffing.

Sausage-Apple Cornbread Dressing: Cook 1 (16-oz.) package ground pork sausage in a large skillet over medium-high heat, stirring often, 8 to 10 minutes or until meat crumbles and is no longer pink; drain. Stir sausage and 2 Granny Smith apples, peeled and diced, into cornbread mixture in Step 1. Proceed as directed.

Green Bean Casserole

Go beyond the standard "recipe on the can" casserole by adding Alfredo sauce for cream of mushroom soup, and adding water chestnuts, Parmesan cheese, and toasted pecans.

makes 10 servings • hands-on time: 15 min. • total time: 4 hr., 45 min.

2 (16-oz.) packages frozen French-cut green beans, thawed

1 (10-oz.) container refrigerated Alfredo sauce

1 (8-oz.) can diced water chestnuts, drained

1 (6-oz.) jar sliced mushrooms, drained

1 cup (4 oz.) shredded Parmesan cheese

½ tsp. freshly ground pepper

1 (6-oz.) can French fried onions, divided

½ cup chopped pecans

1. Stir together first 6 ingredients and half of French fried onions; spoon mixture into a lightly greased 4-qt. slow cooker.

2. Cover and cook on LOW 4½ hours or until bubbly.

3. Heat pecans and remaining French fried onions in a small nonstick skillet over medium-low heat, stirring often, 1 to 2 minutes or until toasted and fragrant; sprinkle over casserole just before serving.

ideal slow cooker
4-quart

Spinach-Artichoke Casserole

Melba rounds make sturdy dippers for serving this dish straight out of the pot.

makes 8 to 10 servings • hands-on time: 20 min. • total time: 4 hr., 20 min.

1	Tbsp. butter
1	(8-oz.) package sliced fresh mushrooms
2	garlic cloves, pressed
1	Tbsp. lemon juice
½	tsp. pepper
2	(10-oz.) packages frozen chopped spinach, thawed
1	(14-oz.) can quartered artichoke hearts, drained and chopped
1	(10¾-oz.) can reduced-fat, reduced-sodium cream of mushroom soup
1	(8-oz.) container reduced-fat sour cream
3	green onions, chopped
2	Tbsp. all-purpose flour
1	Tbsp. chopped fresh parsley
¼	tsp. Worcestershire sauce
2	cups (8 oz.) shredded Monterey Jack cheese with peppers

1. Melt butter in a large skillet over medium-high heat. Add mushrooms and next 3 ingredients; sauté 5 minutes.

2. Meanwhile, drain spinach well, pressing between paper towels. Stir together spinach and next 7 ingredients.

3. Stir mushroom mixture into spinach mixture. Add 1 cup cheese, stirring well. Spoon into a 4-qt. slow cooker. Sprinkle with remaining 1 cup cheese.

4. Cover and cook on HIGH 2 hours or on LOW 4 hours.

Creamy Ranch Cauliflower

If cauliflower is a forgotten vegetable in your home, this recipe is sure to bring it back to your dinner table.

makes 6 servings • hands-on time: 10 min. • total time: 6 hr., 10 min.

1 (11-oz.) can Mexican-style corn, drained

1 (10¾-oz.) can cream of onion soup

1 (8-oz.) container sour cream

1 (8-oz.) container chive-and-onion cream cheese, softened

1 (1-oz.) envelope Ranch-style dressing mix

1 jalapeño pepper, minced

3 (10-oz.) packages fresh cauliflower florets

3 bacon slices, cooked and crumbled (optional)

1. Combine first 6 ingredients in a 4-qt. slow cooker. Add cauliflower, stirring well to coat.

2. Cover and cook on LOW 5½ to 6 hours or until tender.

3. Sprinkle with bacon, if desired.

Corn and Potato Chowder

makes 4 to 6 servings • hands-on time: 15 min. • total time: 8 hr., 15 min.

1   lb. baking potatoes, peeled and cut
     into ¼-inch cubes (about 2 cups)
1   (14¾-oz.) can cream-style corn
1   (14½-oz.) can diced tomatoes
1   (14-oz.) can chicken broth
½   cup chopped onion
½   cup coarsely chopped celery
¾   tsp. dried basil
½   tsp. salt
¼   tsp. pepper
1   bay leaf
1   cup whipping cream
¼   cup butter
4   bacon slices, cooked and
     crumbled
Chopped green onions

1. Stir together first 10 ingredients in a 5-qt. slow cooker. Cover and cook on LOW 8 hours or until potato is tender. Add whipping cream and butter, stirring until butter melts. Discard bay leaf. Ladle chowder into bowls; sprinkle each serving with bacon and chopped green onions.

Make It *Easier*

Cook bacon in the microwave, or substitute packaged fully cooked bacon, prepared according to package directions.

ideal slow cooker
4-quart

Parsnip and Pear Soup

makes 6 to 8 servings • hands-on time: 15 min. • total time: 7 hr., 15 min.

1   Tbsp. olive oil
½   cup refrigerated prechopped
        onion
4   garlic cloves, minced
5   cups chicken broth
2   tsp. chopped fresh rosemary
½   tsp. salt
½   tsp. freshly ground pepper
2   lb. parsnips, peeled and chopped
2   ripe pears, peeled and chopped
½   cup half-and-half
Garnishes: cooked and crumbled
        bacon, fresh rosemary sprigs

1. Heat oil in a large skillet over medium-high heat. Add onion and garlic; sauté 3 minutes or until tender.

2. Combine onion mixture, broth, and next 5 ingredients in a 4-qt. slow cooker. Cover and cook on HIGH 7 hours.

3. Stir half-and-half into soup. Process soup, in batches, in a blender until smooth, stopping to scrape down sides as necessary. Pour soup into bowls. Garnish, if desired.

Secret Ingredient

A parsnip is a hardy root vegetable that enjoys cool climates—it requires frost to convert its starches to sugars and develop its sweet, nutty flavor. Although it bears a striking resemblance to a carrot, a parsnip has pale, cream-colored skin. Its tough, woody texture softens with cooking.

Smoked Chicken-Banana Pepper Soup

makes 8 servings • hands-on time: 12 min. • total time: 6 hr., 22 min.

4   bacon slices
1   (8-oz.) container refrigerated prechopped celery, onion, and bell pepper mix
6   cups low-sodium fat-free chicken broth
2   cups sliced pickled banana peppers
2   Tbsp. juice from banana peppers
1   tsp. ground cumin
½   tsp. dried oregano
½   tsp. salt
½   tsp. pepper
8   plum tomatoes, chopped
1   lb. pulled smoked chicken
1   (14-oz.) package boil-in-bag white rice
Garnish: fresh oregano

1. Cook bacon in a large skillet over medium-high heat 5 to 7 minutes or until crisp; remove bacon, and drain on paper towels, reserving drippings in skillet. Coarsely crumble bacon.

2. Add celery mixture to drippings in skillet; cook, stirring constantly, 5 minutes or until tender. Add chicken broth, stirring to loosen particles from bottom of skillet. Transfer broth mixture to a 5-qt. slow cooker. Stir in bacon, peppers, and next 7 ingredients. Cover and cook on LOW for 6 hours. Stir in rice. Cover and cook 10 minutes or until rice is tender. Garnish, if desired.

Chicken and Rice Soup with Mushrooms

For convenience, use a rotisserie chicken in this soup. The average chicken will yield about 3 cups of chopped cooked meat.

makes 8 servings • hands-on time: 10 min. • total time: 4 hr., 40 min.

1	Tbsp. olive oil
1	cup refrigerated prechopped onion
½	cup refrigerated prechopped celery
1	(8-oz.) package sliced fresh mushrooms
2	garlic cloves, minced
5	cups chicken broth
3	cups chopped cooked chicken
2	Tbsp. chopped fresh parsley
1	tsp. chicken bouillon granules
1	(6-oz.) package long-grain and wild rice mix

1. Heat a large skillet over medium-high heat; add oil. Add onion and next 3 ingredients. Sauté 4 minutes or until vegetables are tender; add 2 cups water, stirring to loosen particles from bottom of skillet. Combine vegetable mixture, broth, and remaining ingredients (including seasoning packet from rice mix) in a 4- or 5-qt. slow cooker. Cover and cook on LOW 4 to 4½ hours or until rice is tender.

Steak Soup

makes 6 servings • hands-on time: 15 min. • total time: 8 hr., 45 min.

2¼ lb. sirloin tip roast, cut into 1-inch cubes

¼ cup all-purpose flour

½ tsp. salt

½ tsp. coarsely ground pepper

2 Tbsp. canola oil

1 (1-oz.) envelope dry onion soup mix

4 cups beef broth

1 Tbsp. tomato paste

1 Tbsp. Worcestershire sauce

2 cups uncooked wide egg noodles

1. Combine first 4 ingredients in a large zip-top plastic freezer bag; seal bag, and shake to coat beef.

2. Sauté beef in hot oil in a Dutch oven over medium-high heat 6 minutes or until browned. Place in a 4-qt. slow cooker. Sprinkle onion soup mix over beef. Whisk together beef broth, tomato paste, and Worcestershire; pour over beef. Cover and cook on LOW 8 hours or until beef is tender.

3. Add noodles to slow cooker; cover and cook 30 minutes or until noodles are done.

Slow-Cooker School

Sirloin tip is a leaner cut than traditional chuck roast. It yields a very tender "fall-apart" texture after the low, slow cooking.

Spicy Marinated Eye of Round

makes 8 to 10 servings • hands-on time: 15 min. • total time: 8 hr., 23 min., including sauce

1   (3- to 5-lb.) eye-of-round roast
½   tsp. salt
¼   tsp. pepper
3   sweet onions, sliced
Spicy Sauce

1. Sprinkle roast with salt and pepper. Place roast and onion in a 5-qt. slow cooker. Stir together ingredients for Spicy Sauce, and pour mixture over uncooked roast.

2. Cover and cook on LOW 8 hours.

3. Remove roast; cool slightly, and cut into thin slices. Return slices to sauce in slow cooker.

Spicy Sauce

makes 7 cups • hands-on time: 8 min. • total time: 8 min.

2   cups ketchup
2   cups water
2   sweet onions, sliced
⅓   cup red wine vinegar
¼   cup firmly packed brown sugar
2   Tbsp. Worcestershire sauce
1   tsp. dry mustard
1   tsp. dried oregano
1   tsp. pepper
½   tsp. garlic powder
½   tsp. chili powder
½   tsp. ground cloves
¼   tsp. ground nutmeg
¼   tsp. hot sauce
1   bay leaf

1. Combine all ingredients.

Onion-Encrusted London Broil

Although many butchers label this particular cut of meat "London broil," thick top round steak is also a common term.

makes 5 servings • hands-on time: 4 min. • total time: 9 hr., 4 min.

1 cup soft, fresh breadcrumbs
1 Tbsp. dried parsley flakes
1 tsp. freshly ground pepper
1 (1-oz.) envelope dry onion soup mix
2½ lb. London broil (at least 2 inches thick)

1. Combine first 4 ingredients in a small bowl. Press crumb mixture onto steak, coating completely. Place steak in a 4-qt. slow cooker. Cover and cook on HIGH 1 hour. Reduce heat to LOW, and cook 8 hours. Slice steak across the grain to serve.

Company Pot Roast

makes 8 to 12 servings • hands-on time: 15 min. • total time: 8 hr., 20 min.

2 (2¼- to 2½-lb.) eye-of-round
roasts, trimmed

2 tsp. salt

1 tsp. freshly ground pepper

1 Tbsp. vegetable oil

1 (1-lb.) package baby carrots

1 (14½-oz.) can petite diced
tomatoes

1 cup chopped celery

1 cup beef broth

½ cup dry red wine

4 garlic cloves, chopped

1 tsp. dried thyme leaves

½ tsp. dried marjoram

¼ cup all-purpose flour

1. Rub roasts evenly with salt and pepper.

2. Brown roasts on all sides in hot oil in a Dutch oven over medium-high heat (about 10 minutes). Place roasts, side by side, in a 6-qt. slow cooker. Add carrots and next 7 ingredients. Cover and cook on LOW 8 hours or until tender.

3. To make gravy, transfer roasts and vegetables to a serving platter; measure drippings, and return to slow cooker. For every cup of drippings, whisk together 1 Tbsp. flour and ¼ cup water. Whisk flour mixture into drippings. Cook, uncovered, on HIGH 5 minutes.

ideal slow cooker
5-quart

Easy Burritos

makes 8 to 10 servings • hands-on time: 30 min. • total time: 8 hr., 42 min., including Pico de Gallo

1   large onion, sliced into rings
1   (3- to 4-lb.) sirloin beef roast
1   (1-oz.) package taco seasoning
      mix
16   (6-inch) flour tortillas
4   cups (16 oz.) shredded Cheddar
      or Monterey Jack cheese
Toppings: diced tomatoes, diced
      onions, sliced jalapeño peppers,
      sour cream, black beans
Pico de Gallo

1. Place onion in a 5-qt. slow cooker; add roast and ½ cup water. Sprinkle taco seasoning mix over top of roast.

2. Cover and cook on LOW 8 hours. Remove roast; shred with 2 forks.

3. Heat tortillas according to package directions. Using a slotted spoon, spoon beef mixture down centers of tortillas; top with cheese and desired toppings, and roll up. Serve with Pico de Gallo.

Slow-Cooker School

If your company runs late, the meat for the burritos holds for quite a while. Keep warm on LOW in the slow cooker, if necessary.

Pico de Gallo

makes 3 cups • hands-on time: 12 min. • total time: 12 min.

3   cups diced plum tomatoes
½   cup diced red onion
⅓   cup chopped fresh cilantro
¼   to ⅓ cup diced jalapeño peppers
⅓   cup fresh lime juice
½   tsp. olive oil
¼   tsp. salt
¼   tsp. black pepper

1. Stir together all ingredients in a medium bowl. Cover and chill until ready to serve.

ideal slow cooker
5-quart

Swiss Steak

makes 4 servings • hands-on time: 15 min. • total time: 8 hr., 15 min.

5 bacon slices, halved
2 (8-oz.) containers refrigerated prechopped celery, onion, and bell pepper mix
2 Tbsp. jarred minced garlic
1¼ lb. bottom round steak (about 1 inch thick), cut into 4 equal portions
⅓ cup all-purpose flour
1½ tsp. salt
¾ tsp. freshly ground pepper
1 (14-oz.) can beef broth
1 (14½-oz.) can diced fire-roasted tomatoes, undrained
1 Tbsp. Worcestershire sauce
1 tsp. dried Italian seasoning
Mashed potatoes

1. Cook bacon in a large nonstick skillet over medium-high heat 5 to 6 minutes or until crisp; remove bacon, and drain on paper towels, reserving drippings in skillet. Crumble bacon; set aside. Cook celery mix and garlic in hot drippings, stirring often, until tender. Transfer vegetables to a 5-qt. slow cooker, using a slotted spoon. Reserve drippings in pan.

2. Place meat on a sheet of plastic wrap; flatten with the pointed side of a meat mallet to ¼-inch thickness. Combine flour, salt, and pepper in a shallow dish. Dredge meat in flour mixture; cook in hot drippings 3 minutes on each side or until browned.

3. Place meat in slow cooker over vegetables, reserving drippings in skillet. Add beef broth and next 3 ingredients to skillet, stirring to loosen particles from bottom of skillet. Pour broth mixture over beef in slow cooker. Cover and cook on LOW 8 hours or until beef is very tender. Serve over mashed potatoes. Sprinkle with crumbled bacon before serving.

ideal slow cooker
4- or 5-quart

Beef with Olives

makes 8 to 10 servings • hands-on time: 15 min. • total time: 5 hr., 15 min.

½ cup butter, melted
3 lb. boneless top sirloin steak, cut into 1½-inch pieces
¼ tsp. salt
½ tsp. pepper
1 Tbsp. olive oil
3 large garlic cloves, sliced
2 shallots, vertically sliced
2 cups pimiento-stuffed Spanish olives
2 Tbsp. olive juice from jar
1 (12-oz.) jar roasted red bell peppers, drained and cut into thick strips
Hot cooked yellow rice

1. Pour melted butter into a 4- or 5-qt. slow cooker.

2. Sprinkle beef with salt and pepper. Heat oil in a large skillet over medium-high heat. Cook beef, in 2 batches, 2 minutes on each side. Place beef in slow cooker. Add garlic and shallots to skillet; sauté 1 minute over medium-high heat. Spoon over beef in slow cooker. Coarsely chop 1 cup olives. Sprinkle chopped and whole olives and olive juice over beef.

3. Cover and cook on LOW 5 hours or until beef is tender. Stir in roasted bell peppers just before serving. Serve over hot cooked yellow rice.

Osso Buco

makes 6 servings • hands-on time: 12 min. • total time: 8 hr., 12 min.

2   Tbsp. olive oil, divided
1   (8-oz.) container refrigerated
      prechopped celery, onion, and
      bell pepper mix
½   cup chopped carrot
3   garlic cloves, minced
6   (1½- to 2-inch-thick) veal shanks
      (about 4 lb.)
1   tsp. salt, divided
½   tsp. freshly ground pepper
¾   cup all-purpose flour, divided
½   cup dry white wine
2   (14½-oz.) cans diced tomatoes
      with basil, garlic, and oregano
1   (14-oz.) can beef broth
Hot cooked polenta
Chopped fresh parsley (optional)

1. Heat 1 Tbsp. oil in a large skillet over medium-high heat. Add celery mix and carrot; sauté 3 minutes or until tender. Add garlic; sauté 1 minute or until tender. Transfer vegetable mixture to a lightly greased 5- or 6-qt. slow cooker.

2. Sprinkle veal with ½ tsp. salt and pepper. Dredge veal in ½ cup plus 1 Tbsp. flour; shake off excess. Heat remaining 1 Tbsp. oil in skillet over medium-high heat. Add veal; cook 3 to 4 minutes on each side or until browned. Arrange veal over vegetables in slow cooker. Add wine to drippings in skillet, stirring to loosen particles from bottom of skillet. Stir in tomatoes, broth, remaining 3 Tbsp. flour, and remaining ½ tsp. salt. Pour over veal in slow cooker.

3. Cover and cook on LOW 8 hours or until veal is very tender (meat will fall off the bone). Cover and set aside until ready to serve. Serve over polenta. Sprinkle with parsley, if desired.

Garlic Lamb Shanks with Tomato Gravy

makes 4 servings • hands-on time: 15 min. • total time: 10 hr., 15 min.

1	Tbsp. olive oil
4	lamb shanks (4 lb.), trimmed
1	cup dry white wine
2	Tbsp. honey
2	Tbsp. coarse-grained mustard
1	Tbsp. fresh thyme leaves
1	Tbsp. lemon zest
1	tsp. salt
½	tsp. freshly ground pepper
1	(14½-oz.) can stewed tomatoes
4	garlic bulbs, unpeeled and separated into cloves
Hot cooked couscous	
2	Tbsp. chopped fresh parsley

1. Heat oil in a large skillet over medium-high heat. Brown lamb 4 minutes on each side. Transfer lamb to a 6-qt. slow cooker. Add wine and next 8 ingredients to skillet, stirring to loosen particles from bottom of skillet. Bring to a boil; pour over lamb.

2. Cover and cook on LOW 10 hours or until lamb is very tender. Serve over couscous. Sprinkle with parsley.

Secret Ingredient

Thyme, a congenial herb, pairs well with many other herbs—especially rosemary, parsley, sage, savory, and oregano. Because the leaves are so small, they often don't require chopping.

ideal slow cooker
5-quart

Pork Carnitas Nachos

makes 4 servings • hands-on time: 10 min. • total time: 6 hr., 10 min.

1 onion, sliced

2 Tbsp. chopped canned chipotle peppers in adobo sauce or 2 fresh jalapeño peppers, seeded and sliced

2- to 3-lb. boned pork butt or shoulder

4 garlic cloves, slivered

Salt and pepper to taste

1 Tbsp. vegetable oil

Tortilla chips

Toppings: jalapeños, shredded Monterey Jack cheese, salsa verde, fresh salsa

1. Combine onion, chipotle or jalapeño peppers, and ¼ cup water in a 5-qt. slow cooker. Using a knife, make slits all over pork, and insert garlic into slits. Season roast with salt and pepper. Heat a large Dutch oven over medium-high heat; add oil. Brown roast on all sides, about 8 minutes. Transfer roast to slow cooker. Pour ½ cup water into Dutch oven; stir over low heat with a wooden spoon to loosen browned particles from bottom of Dutch oven. Pour liquid into slow cooker. Cover and cook on HIGH 6 hours.

2. Remove roast from slow cooker; let cool. Shred pork using 2 forks. Return pulled pork to slow cooker, stirring to combine. Serve pork over tortilla chips with desired toppings.

**ideal slow cooker
6-quart**

Red Wine-Braised Short Ribs

You can also serve this hearty recipe over mashed potatoes or polenta.

makes 6 servings • hands-on time: 10 min. • total time: 8 hr., 10 min.

2 medium onions, cut into wedges

4 garlic cloves, peeled and crushed

6 small carrots, peeled and cut in half crosswise

2 small parsnips, peeled and cut into quarters crosswise

1 oz. dried porcini mushrooms, rinsed

1 (8½-oz.) jar sun-dried tomatoes, drained and cut in half lengthwise

1 small bunch sage

5 lb. beef short ribs

1½ tsp. kosher salt

¾ tsp. pepper

1 bottle red wine

Garnish: fresh sage sprigs

1. Combine onion, garlic, carrots, parsnips, mushrooms, tomatoes, and sage in a 6-qt. slow cooker. Season short ribs with salt and pepper, and nestle them among vegetables. Add wine. Cover and cook on HIGH 8 hours or until meat is tender and falls off the bones. Using a large spoon, skim off excess fat and discard. Divide ribs and vegetables among shallow bowls, and spoon sauce over top. Garnish, if desired.

Chicken Paprikash

makes 6 servings • hands-on time: 12 min. • total time: 7 hr., 12 min.

3   Tbsp. all-purpose flour
2   lb. skinned and boned chicken breasts, cut into ½-inch strips
2   cups chopped onion
1¼ cups low-sodium fat-free chicken broth
1   cup chopped red bell pepper
½   cup shredded carrot
2   Tbsp. Hungarian sweet paprika
2   tsp. jarred minced garlic
1   tsp. salt
1   tsp. freshly ground black pepper
1   (8-oz.) package sliced mushrooms
1¼ cups sour cream
Hot cooked orzo

1. Combine flour and chicken in a medium bowl; toss well. Add chicken mixture, chopped onion, and next 8 ingredients to a 4-qt. slow cooker. Cover and cook on HIGH 1 hour. Reduce heat to LOW, and cook 6 hours. Stir in sour cream. Serve over hot cooked orzo.

Chicken Parmesan

makes 6 servings • hands-on time: 12 min. • total time: 3 hr., 47 min.

2   cups Italian-seasoned Japanese breadcrumbs (panko)
6   skinned and boned chicken breasts
2   large eggs, lightly beaten
4   Tbsp. olive oil
1   (44-oz.) jar tomato-basil pasta sauce
¾   tsp. salt
½   tsp. pepper
1   (8-oz.) package shredded mozzarella cheese
¾   cup (3 oz.) shredded Parmesan cheese
Cooked spaghetti
Garnish: fresh oregano

1. Spread breadcrumbs on a large plate. Dip chicken in beaten egg, 1 breast at a time. Dredge chicken in breadcrumbs, pressing crumbs gently to adhere.

2. Heat 2 Tbsp. oil in a large nonstick skillet over medium-high heat. Cook chicken, in 2 batches, 2 minutes on each side or until browned, adding remaining 2 Tbsp. oil with second batch.

3. Pour pasta sauce into a lightly greased 6- or 7-qt. oval slow cooker. Arrange chicken in slow cooker over sauce. Sprinkle with salt and pepper. Cover and cook on HIGH 3½ hours. Add cheeses; cover and cook on HIGH 5 more minutes or until cheese melts. Serve over spaghetti. Garnish, if desired.

Secret Ingredient

Crunchy panko breadcrumbs are a Japanese secret that we use to make foods crisp without deep-frying. These Asian-style breadcrumbs are coarser than the American version, and so create a crunchy crust that can be just as satisfying as the crust on a deep-fried food. Panko breadcrumbs are available in most regular grocery stores.

ideal slow cooker
5-quart oval

Chicken with Artichokes and Wild Mushrooms

makes 4 servings • hands-on time: 15 min. • total time: 4 hr., 15 min.

2 skinned, bone-in chicken breasts
2 chicken drumsticks
2 skinned, bone-in chicken thighs
3 Tbsp. all-purpose flour
1 tsp. salt
½ tsp. freshly ground pepper
3 Tbsp. olive oil
2 (4-oz.) packages assorted wild mushrooms
2¾ cups vertically sliced Vidalia or other sweet onion
1 cup chicken broth
3 Tbsp. drained capers
1 (12-oz.) jar marinated artichoke hearts, undrained
Garnish: fresh oregano leaves

1. Rinse chicken, and pat dry. Combine flour, salt, and pepper in a large zip-top plastic freezer bag. Place chicken pieces in bag; seal bag, and shake to coat. Remove chicken.

2. Heat oil in a large skillet over medium-high heat until hot; add chicken. Cook 3 minutes on each side or until lightly browned. Place in a greased 5-qt. oval slow cooker, reserving drippings in skillet.

3. Cook mushrooms and onion in hot drippings 5 minutes or until tender. Add mushroom mixture, broth, capers, and artichoke hearts to slow cooker. Cover and cook on LOW 4 hours or until chicken is tender. Garnish, if desired.

Chicken Marsala

makes 8 servings • hands-on time: 20 min. • total time: 6 hr., 30 min.

2 cloves garlic, finely chopped

1 Tbsp. vegetable oil

8 skinned and boned chicken breasts

½ tsp. salt

½ tsp. pepper

2 (6-oz.) jars sliced mushrooms, drained

1 cup sweet Marsala wine or chicken broth

¼ cup cornstarch

Hot cooked rice

Garnish: chopped fresh parsley

1. Mix garlic and oil in a lightly greased 4- or 5-qt. slow cooker. Sprinkle chicken with salt and pepper; place over garlic. Place mushrooms over chicken; pour wine over all.

2. Cover and cook on LOW 5 to 6 hours.

3. Remove chicken from slow cooker; cover to keep warm. In small bowl, mix ½ cup water and cornstarch until smooth; stir into liquid in slow cooker. Increase heat to HIGH. Cover and cook about 10 minutes or until sauce is slightly thickened.

4. Return chicken to slow cooker. Cover and cook on HIGH 5 minutes or until hot. Serve over rice. Garnish, if desired.

ideal slow cooker
3½- or 4-quart oval

Turkey Meatball Stroganoff

makes 6 servings • hands-on time: 20 min. • total time: 7 hr., 35 min.

1	lb. lean ground turkey
½	cup soft breadcrumbs
½	cup finely chopped onion
1	tsp. country-style Dijon mustard
½	tsp. salt
½	tsp. freshly ground pepper
2	(8-oz.) packages fresh mushrooms, quartered
1	(14-oz.) can low-sodium beef broth
5	cups uncooked wide egg noodles
⅓	cup all-purpose flour
⅓	cup cold water
1	(12-oz.) container light French onion dip

Garnish: chopped fresh parsley

1. In medium bowl, mix turkey, breadcrumbs, onion, mustard, salt, and pepper. Shape mixture into 16 meatballs, and add to a lightly greased medium nonstick skillet. Cook over medium-high heat until brown. Place meatballs in a lightly greased 3½- or 4-qt. oval slow cooker; top with mushrooms. Add broth.

2. Cover and cook on LOW 6 to 7 hours.

3. Prepare noodles according to package directions. Remove meatballs and mushrooms from slow cooker using slotted spoon; cover to keep warm. In small bowl, mix flour and water; gradually stir into slow cooker until blended. Increase heat to HIGH. Cover and cook on HIGH 15 to 20 minutes or until thickened. Stir in dip; heat until hot. Stir in meatballs and mushrooms. Serve over noodles. Garnish, if desired.

Barbecued Shrimp

makes 4 servings • hands-on time: 5 min. • total time: 2 hr., 50 min. • pictured on page 78

6   garlic cloves, pressed
1   cup butter, divided
½   cup Worcestershire sauce
¼   cup fresh lemon juice
¼   cup cocktail sauce
1   Tbsp. freshly ground pepper
1½ Tbsp. Old Bay seasoning
1   tsp. paprika
1   tsp. dried Italian seasoning
2   lb. unpeeled, large raw shrimp
    (21/25 count)
1   lemon, sliced
Hot sauce (optional)
Lemon wedges (optional)
2   French bread baguettes, sliced

1. Sauté garlic in ¼ cup butter in a skillet over medium-high heat 2 minutes or until fragrant and lightly browned. Remove from heat; spoon into a 6-qt. oval slow cooker. Add remaining ¾ cup butter and next 7 ingredients. Cover and cook on LOW 2 hours.

2. Add shrimp and sliced lemon. Increase heat to HIGH. Cover and cook on HIGH 45 minutes or until shrimp turn pink, stirring once after 30 minutes. Add hot sauce, if desired. Serve with lemon wedges, if desired, and bread.

ideal slow cooker
3½-quart

Seafood Pot Pie

makes 6 servings • hands-on time: 15 min. • total time: 3 hr., 15 min.

Parchment paper
¼ cup butter
1 cup chopped onion or 1 leek, thinly sliced
2 tsp. jarred minced garlic
1 (8-oz.) package sliced baby portobello mushrooms
¼ cup all-purpose flour
1 cup half-and-half
1 cup chicken broth
1 (11-oz.) package frozen baby broccoli blend
½ lb. fresh lump crabmeat, drained
1 (1-lb.) cod fillet, cut into 2-inch pieces
½ tsp. salt
½ tsp. freshly ground pepper
½ (17.3-oz.) package frozen puff pastry sheets, thawed
1 egg yolk, beaten
¼ cup dry sherry

1. To make a template for pastry lid, place a 3½-qt. slow-cooker lid on parchment paper; trace lid shape. Remove lid. Cut out parchment shape, and set aside.

2. Melt butter in a large skillet over medium-high heat. Add onion or leek, garlic, and mushrooms; sauté 5 minutes. Whisk in flour until smooth. Cook 1 minute, whisking constantly. Gradually whisk in half-and-half and broth; cook over medium heat, whisking constantly, until thickened and bubbly. Transfer to a slow cooker. Stir in broccoli blend. Cover and cook on LOW 2 hours. Pick crabmeat, removing any bits of shell. Uncover and stir in crabmeat, cod, salt, and pepper (cooker will be almost full). Cover and cook on HIGH 1 hour or until cod flakes easily with a fork.

3. Preheat oven to 400°. Roll out 1 pastry sheet on a lightly floured surface until smooth. Place parchment template on pastry, and cut out pastry using a paring knife. Place pastry on a parchment paper-lined baking sheet. Brush with egg yolk. Bake at 400° for 14 to 15 minutes. Stir sherry into pot pie. Top pot pie with pastry lid just before serving. Serve hot.

How to Cut Leeks

Trim the root portion just above the base. Slice off and discard the fibrous green tops, leaving only the white-to-light-green stalk. Cut the leek in half lengthwise, and then cut it according to your recipe.

Chocolate-Butterscotch Lava Cake

makes 12 servings • hands-on time: 20 min. • total time: 4 hr., 50 min.

1 (17.5-oz.) package dark chocolate cake mix

1 (3.4-oz.) package chocolate instant pudding and pie filling mix

1 cup sour cream

⅓ cup butter, melted

1 tsp. vanilla

3¼ cups milk, divided

3 eggs

1 (8-oz.) package toffee bits, divided

1 (3.4-oz.) package butterscotch instant pudding and pie filling mix

1 (8-oz.) container frozen whipped topping, thawed

1. In a large bowl, beat cake mix, chocolate pudding mix, sour cream, butter, vanilla, 1¼ cups milk, and eggs at medium speed of an electric mixer 2 minutes, scraping down sides of bowl as needed. Stir in 1 cup of the toffee bits. Pour batter into a lightly greased 5-qt. oval slow cooker.

2. In a medium saucepan, heat remaining 2 cups milk over medium heat 3 to 5 minutes, stirring frequently, until hot and bubbly. Remove from heat. Sprinkle butterscotch pudding mix over batter in slow cooker. Slowly pour hot milk over pudding.

3. Cover and cook on LOW 4½ hours or until edge of cake is set at least 2 inches from edge of slow cooker, but center still jiggles slightly when moved. Turn off slow cooker. Let stand 15 minutes. Top with whipped topping and remaining toffee bits.

Cranberry Upside-Down Cake

Here's a festive twist on traditional pineapple upside-down cake. Serve with ice cream or sweetened whipped cream to complement the tartness of the cranberries.

makes 8 to 10 servings • hands-on time: 10 min. • total time: 2 hr., 40 min.

1   cup firmly packed light brown sugar
½   cup butter, melted
1   (14-oz.) can whole-berry cranberry sauce
1   (12-oz.) package fresh cranberries
1   (16-oz.) package pound cake mix
¾   cup milk
2   large eggs
½   tsp. almond extract

1. Stir together first 3 ingredients in a small bowl until blended. Pour mixture into a lightly greased 5-qt. slow cooker. Top with cranberries.

2. Beat pound cake mix, milk, and next 2 ingredients at low speed with an electric mixer 30 seconds, scraping bowl constantly. Beat at low speed for an additional 2 minutes. Pour batter over cranberries. Cover and cook on HIGH 2 hours and 10 minutes or until a wooden pick inserted in center comes out clean. Turn off slow cooker; let cake stand, covered, 20 minutes. Invert cake onto a serving platter.

Bittersweet Fudge Brownie Bread Pudding

makes 8 to 10 servings • hands-on time: 15 min. • total time: 3 hr., 25 min.

1   (18-oz.) package double chocolate brownie mix

8   large eggs

¾   cup sugar

1   Tbsp. vanilla extract or vanilla bean paste

Pinch of salt

3   cups heavy cream

1   (1-lb.) loaf ciabatta bread, cut into 1-inch cubes (about 8 cups)

1   (10-oz.) package bittersweet chocolate morsels

1   cup pecan halves, toasted (optional)

1   slow-cooker liner

Cooking spray

1. Prepare and bake brownies according to package directions. Cool completely, and cut into 1½-inch chunks to measure 4 cups packed, reserving remaining brownies for another use. Cover and set aside up to 1 day ahead.

2. Whisk together eggs and next 3 ingredients in a large bowl; whisk in cream until blended. Stir in bread and 4 cups brownie chunks. Stir in chocolate morsels and, if desired, nuts.

3. Place liner in a 5-qt. round slow cooker according to manufacturer's instructions. Heavily coat liner with cooking spray. Spoon bread mixture into liner. Cover and cook on HIGH 3 hours or until pudding is set in center, rotating slow cooker insert twice to prevent overbrowning of bottom edge. Turn off slow cooker; let stand, uncovered, 10 minutes. Serve warm.

Make it *Easier*

Your favorite fudgy brownies will also work fine in this recipe. You need just 4 cups of brownie chunks. If you're in a hurry, pick up brownies at the bakery.

Pomegranate Spiced Tea

Substitute loose tea for the tea bags: Spoon 2 Tbsp. tea leaves into a large tea ball, and place the tea ball in the slow cooker.

makes 10 cups • hands-on time: 10 min. • total time: 4 hr., 10 min.

8	cups cold water
1	(16-oz.) bottle pomegranate juice
¾	cup sugar
2	cinnamon sticks (2- to 3-inch)
2	tsp. whole allspice
½	tsp. whole cloves
6	tea bags black tea

Garnish: lemon slices

1. Stir together water, pomegranate juice, and sugar in a 4- or 5-qt. slow cooker until sugar is dissolved. Add cinnamon sticks, allspice, and cloves. Cut paper label from tea bags. Tie strings of bags together to keep bags attached; place in slow cooker.

2. Cover and cook on HIGH 4 hours. Remove tea bags; remove spices with a small strainer before serving. Garnish, if desired.

Extreme Hot Chocolate

makes 12 cups • hands-on time: 6 min. • total time: 4 hr., 6 min.

1 (12-oz.) can evaporated milk
1 cup instant nonfat dry milk
4½ cups milk
3 cups whipping cream
⅛ tsp. salt
1 (10-oz.) package bittersweet chocolate morsels
1 (12-oz.) package semisweet chocolate morsels
1 (10-oz.) package large marshmallows
Parchment paper
1 Tbsp. vanilla extract
Coffee liqueur (optional)

1. Whisk together evaporated milk and dry milk in a 4-qt. slow cooker until smooth. Whisk in milk and next 2 ingredients. Add chocolate morsels. Cover and cook on LOW 4 hours, whisking until smooth after 2 hours.

2. Preheat broiler with oven rack 3 inches from heat. Place 12 marshmallows on a parchment paper-lined baking sheet. Broil 2 minutes or until toasted. Repeat procedure with desired amount of marshmallows. Stir vanilla into hot chocolate, and ladle into mugs. Stir 1 Tbsp. liqueur into each serving, if desired, and top each serving with 1 to 2 toasted marshmallows.

Slow-Cooker School

Known for cooking hot beverages to perfection, slow cookers are great for entertaining, because they will keep the liquid warm throughout the party.

Spirited Hot Mocha

Serve this coffee-flavored hot chocolate straight from the slow cooker. Brandy adds a spirited punch, but you can omit it, if desired.

makes 10 cups • hands-on time: 2 min. • total time: 5 hr., 2 min.

8　cups milk

1　(6-oz.) package semisweet chocolate mini-morsels or 6 (1-oz.) semisweet chocolate baking squares, chopped

½　cup powdered sugar

¼　cup instant coffee granules

1　cup brandy

Sweetened whipped cream (optional)

Grated semisweet chocolate (optional)

1. Combine first 5 ingredients in a 4-qt. slow cooker.

2. Cover and cook on LOW 4 to 5 hours or until thoroughly heated and chocolate is melted, whisking after 2 hours. Whisk again before serving. Serve with sweetened whipped cream and grated semisweet chocolate, if desired.

Caramel Apple Cider

This cider is perfect for a party because it can be cooked and served out of the slow cooker.

makes 8 cups • hands-on time: 5 min. • total time: 4 hr., 5 min.

1   (64-oz.) bottle apple cider
⅓   cup caramel topping
½   tsp. ground cinnamon
Fresh whipped cream
Additional ground cinnamon
Additional caramel topping
Garnish: cinnamon sticks

1. Combine first 3 ingredients in a 3-qt. slow cooker.

2. Cover and cook on LOW 3 to 4 hours. Ladle into individual mugs, and dollop with whipped cream; sprinkle with cinnamon. Drizzle with additional caramel topping. Garnish, if desired.

Beer and Sharp Cheddar Soup with
Baguette Toasts, page 143

Party in
a Pot

Mexican Corn Pudding

makes 8 servings • hands-on time: 21 min. • total time: 5 hr., 26 min.

2   large eggs
1   (15¼-oz.) can whole kernel corn
1   (14¾-oz.) can cream-style corn
1   (4½-oz.) can diced green chiles
1   (8½-oz.) package corn muffin mix
½   cup butter, melted
1   tsp. cumin
Garnish: fresh cilantro

1. Whisk eggs in a large bowl. Add next 6 ingredients, and mix well. Pour into a lightly greased 3-qt. oval slow cooker.

2. Cover and cook on LOW 5 hours or until edges are set. Let stand 5 minutes. Stir before serving. Garnish, if desired.

Note: We tested with "Jiffy" corn muffin mix.

Slow-Cooker School

Cheese can add extra "yum" to vegetable dishes cooked in the slow cooker by adding it at the end of cooking time. In this particular recipe, add ¼ cup cheese of your choice at the end of the cooking time. Cover and cook for 10 more minutes or until the cheese is melted; then serve.

Burgundy Mushrooms

makes 8 servings • hands-on time: 15 min. • total time: 8 hr., 15 min.

3 lb. fresh mushrooms
1½ cups Burgundy or other dry red wine
1 (14-oz.) can beef broth
½ cup butter, cut into pieces
1 Tbsp. Worcestershire sauce
1 tsp. salt
½ tsp. garlic powder
½ tsp. dried thyme
½ tsp. pepper
Garnish: fresh thyme sprigs

1. Place mushrooms in a 6-qt. slow cooker. Add Burgundy and remaining ingredients except garnish to slow cooker.

2. Cover and cook on LOW 8 hours. Serve with a slotted spoon. Garnish, if desired.

Slow-Cooker School

The delicious juices left over after cooking the mushrooms can be used for a multitude of other dishes. Try thickening 1½ cups liquid with 1½ tablespoons all-purpose flour for a tasty sauce with French dip sandwiches. You can also pour the juices into ice-cube trays, freeze, and pop them out later to flavor soups or vegetables.

Ratatouille

makes 8 to 10 servings • hands-on time: 20 min. • total time: 8 hr., 20 min.

1	large eggplant, peeled and cut into 1-inch cubes (about 1½ lb.)
1	large onion, chopped
2	tomatoes, chopped
1	large green bell pepper, cut into ½-inch pieces
1	large red bell pepper, cut into ½-inch pieces
3	medium zucchini, chopped
3	garlic cloves, minced
3	Tbsp. olive oil
1	Tbsp. capers
1	tsp. salt
½	tsp. black pepper
¼	cup tomato paste
1	(4½-oz.) can sliced black olives, drained
¼	cup chopped fresh basil
½	cup shaved Parmesan cheese

1. Combine first 11 ingredients in a 6-qt. slow cooker.

2. Cover and cook on LOW 8 hours.

3. Stir in tomato paste, olives, and basil. Sprinkle each serving with cheese.

Loaded Potato Soup

makes 8 servings • hands-on time: 15 min. • total time: 8 hr., 35 min.

4 lb. new potatoes, peeled and cut into ¼-inch-thick slices

1 small onion, chopped

2 (14-oz.) cans chicken broth

2 tsp. salt

½ tsp. pepper

2 cups half-and-half

Toppings: shredded Cheddar cheese, cooked and crumbled bacon, sliced green onions

1. Layer sliced potatoes in a lightly greased 5-qt. slow cooker; top with chopped onion.

2. Stir together broth, salt, and pepper; pour over potatoes and onion. (Broth will not completely cover potatoes and onion.) Cover and cook on LOW 8 hours or until potatoes are tender. Mash mixture with a potato masher; stir in half-and-half. Cover and cook on HIGH 20 more minutes or until mixture is thoroughly heated. Ladle into bowls, and serve with desired toppings.

How to Peel Potatoes

Peeling potatoes yields a softer texture, which is ideal for this creamy soup. You can easily remove the skin from a potato using a vegetable peeler.

French Onion Soup

This soup makes a large volume and freezes well if not eaten all at once.

makes 8 to 10 servings • hands-on time: 8 min. • total time: 8 hr., 23 min.

6   large sweet onions, thinly sliced
¼   cup butter, melted
½   tsp. salt
½   tsp. freshly ground pepper
1   (32-oz.) container beef broth
2   (10½-oz.) cans beef consommé
¼   cup dry white wine
1   tsp. fresh thyme leaves
8   to 10 (½-inch-thick) French bread
      baguette slices
½   cup (2 oz.) shredded Gruyère
      cheese
Garnish: fresh thyme

1. Combine first 4 ingredients in a lightly greased 5- or 6-qt. slow cooker. Cover and cook on LOW 8 hours.

2. Stir broth and next 3 ingredients into onion mixture. Cover and cook 15 more minutes or until hot.

3. Meanwhile, preheat broiler with oven rack 3 inches from heat. Sprinkle baguette slices with shredded cheese; place on a lightly greased baking sheet. Broil 1 to 2 minutes or until cheese melts. Serve soup with cheese toasts. Garnish, if desired.

Beer and Sharp Cheddar Soup with Baguette Toasts

makes 6 servings • hands-on time: 6 min. • total time: 2 hr., 51 min. • pictured on page 134

⅓ cup butter

1½ cups refrigerated prechopped celery, onion, and bell pepper mix

2 carrots, chopped

1 Tbsp. jarred minced garlic

½ cup all-purpose flour

2 cups half-and-half

1 cup chicken broth

3 cups (12 oz.) shredded sharp Cheddar cheese

1 (12-oz.) can beer

Salt and pepper to taste

1 Tbsp. Worcestershire sauce (optional)

Baguette Toasts

1. Melt butter in a large saucepan over medium-high heat. Add celery mix, carrot, and garlic; sauté 5 to 6 minutes or just until tender. Whisk in flour until smooth. Cook 1 minute, stirring constantly. Gradually whisk in half-and-half and broth; cook over medium heat, whisking constantly, 3 to 4 minutes or until thickened and bubbly. Transfer to a 4-qt. slow cooker. Stir in cheese and beer. Cover and cook on LOW 2½ hours. Season to taste with salt and pepper. Add Worcestershire sauce, if desired. Serve with Baguette Toasts.

Baguette Toasts

makes 6 servings • hands-on time: 5 min. • total time: 8 min.

½ (8.5-oz.) French bread baguette

1 garlic bulb (optional)

Paprika (optional)

Olive oil cooking spray

1. Preheat oven to 450°. Cut baguette diagonally into ½-inch slices. Separate garlic cloves. Rub baguette slices with cut garlic cloves, if desired. Dust slices with paprika, if desired. Arrange baguette slices on a baking sheet; coat with cooking spray. Bake at 450° for 3 to 4 minutes or until toasted.

15-Bean and Tomato Soup

makes 12 servings • hands-on time: 14 min. • total time: 18 hr., 14 min.

1 (20-oz.) package 15-bean soup mix
4 bacon slices
2 cups refrigerated prechopped onion
½ cup chopped carrot (about 1 small)
2 garlic cloves, pressed
½ tsp. chopped fresh rosemary
¼ tsp. salt
¼ tsp. freshly ground pepper
2 (32-oz.) containers chicken broth
2 (14½-oz.) cans diced tomatoes with balsamic vinegar, basil, and oil, undrained
Garnishes: shaved Parmesan, fresh rosemary

1. Rinse and sort bean mix according to package directions. Place bean mix in a 6-qt. slow cooker, reserving seasoning packet for another use. Cover with water 2 inches above bean mix; let soak 8 hours. Drain and return to slow cooker.

2. Cook bacon in a large skillet over medium-high heat 5 to 7 minutes or until crisp. Remove bacon, and drain on paper towels; reserve drippings in skillet. Crumble bacon. Sauté onion and carrot in hot drippings 3 minutes or until tender. Add garlic; sauté 1 minute.

3. Stir bacon, vegetable mixture, rosemary, and remaining ingredients except garnishes into bean mix in slow cooker. Cover and cook on LOW 10 hours or until beans are tender. Garnish, if desired.

ideal slow cooker
5-quart

Smokehouse Chicken and Vegetable Stew

makes 8 servings • hands-on time: 5 min. • total time: 8 hr., 5 min.

1 cup chicken broth

½ cup sweet-and-spicy barbecue sauce

1¼ cups refrigerated prechopped tricolor bell pepper

1 cup frozen baby lima beans

2 Tbsp. Worcestershire sauce

½ tsp. salt

½ tsp. pepper

2 lb. pulled smoked chicken

1 (26-oz.) jar fire-roasted tomato and garlic pasta sauce

1 (16-oz.) package frozen mixed vegetables

1 (8-oz.) container refrigerated prechopped onion

1. Combine all ingredients in a 5-qt. slow cooker. Cover and cook on HIGH 8 hours.

Slow-Cooker School

Don't be tempted to add more liquid to the slow cooker; as the vegetables cook, they release enough liquid to make this thick stew the right consistency.

African Lamb-Peanut Stew

We used frozen cut sweet potatoes to eliminate the time-consuming task of peeling and cubing the potatoes.

makes 10 servings • hands-on time: 15 min. • total time: 9 hr.

1½ lb. boneless lean lamb, cut into 1-inch pieces
1 tsp. salt, divided
¼ tsp. freshly ground pepper
2 Tbsp. olive oil
2 (14½-oz.) cans diced tomatoes with garlic and onion, undrained
2 large jalapeño peppers, minced
1 (8-oz.) container refrigerated prechopped onion
2 garlic cloves, minced
5 cups chicken broth
¾ cup creamy peanut butter
2 Tbsp. tomato paste
1 (24-oz.) package steam-and-mash frozen cut sweet potatoes
2 cups frozen cut okra
Hot cooked couscous
Garnish: chopped fresh parsley

1. Sprinkle lamb with ½ tsp. salt and pepper. Cook lamb in hot oil in a large skillet over medium-high heat, stirring often, 5 minutes or until browned on all sides. Drain. Place in a 6-qt. slow cooker.

2. Add tomatoes and next 3 ingredients to slow cooker. Whisk together broth, remaining ½ tsp. salt, peanut butter, and tomato paste; pour over vegetables and lamb. Cover and cook on LOW 8 hours. Stir in sweet potatoes and okra. Cook 45 more minutes or until vegetables are tender. Serve with couscous. Garnish, if desired.

ideal slow cooker
5- or 6-quart

Beef and Chicken Fajitas

makes 10 servings • hands-on time: 15 min. • total time: 7 hr., 15 min.

1½ lb. flat-iron steak, cut into strips
1 lb. skinned and boned chicken breasts, cut into strips
1 tsp. salt
1 tsp. pepper
1½ Tbsp. fajita seasoning, divided
4 Tbsp. olive oil, divided
3 Tbsp. fresh lime juice
2 Tbsp. Worcestershire sauce
5 large garlic cloves, minced
1½ (1-lb.) packages frozen pepper stir-fry
10 (8-inch) flour tortillas, warmed
Lime wedges (optional)
Toppings: guacamole, shredded lettuce, chopped tomato, shredded Cheddar cheese

1. Place steak and chicken strips on separate plates; sprinkle with salt, pepper, and 1 Tbsp. fajita seasoning.

2. Heat 1 Tbsp. oil in an extra-large skillet over medium-high heat. Add steak to pan; cook 3 minutes or until browned, turning once. Place steak in a 5- or 6-qt. slow cooker. Add chicken to pan; cook over medium-high heat 3 minutes or until browned, stirring once. Add chicken to steak in slow cooker.

3. Stir together remaining 3 Tbsp. oil, lime juice, Worcestershire sauce, garlic, and remaining 1½ tsp. fajita seasoning in a medium bowl; pour over chicken and steak in slow cooker. Cover and cook on LOW 5 hours or until meat is tender. Stir in frozen pepper stir-fry. Cover and cook 1 to 2 more hours.

4. Spoon filling into tortillas and, if desired, squeeze lime wedges over filling. Serve with desired toppings.

How to Peel & Mince Garlic

1. To loosen the papery skin of the garlic, place the flat side of a chef's knife on an unpeeled garlic clove. To crush, press down using the heel of your hand. **2.** Peel off the skin. Remove the tough end with a knife. **3.** To mince, make lengthwise cuts through the clove, and then cut the strips crosswise for chopped or minced pieces.

ideal slow cooker
5-quart

Beef Tacos

Brown the beef before slow cooking to add color and enhance flavor. This mixture is also great over baked potatoes with your favorite toppings.

makes 8 servings • hands-on time: 15 min. • total time: 8 hr., 15 min.

2   lb. boneless beef chuck roast, cut into 1-inch cubes
1   tsp. salt
1   Tbsp. vegetable oil
1   Tbsp. chili powder
1   (6-oz.) can tomato paste
2   cups beef broth
1   small white onion, sliced
1   (8-oz.) can tomato sauce
½   medium-size green bell pepper
1   tsp. ground cumin
½   tsp. pepper
8   taco shells
Toppings: shredded Cheddar cheese, shredded lettuce, fresh salsa

1. Sprinkle beef with salt.

2. Cook beef in hot oil in a Dutch oven over medium-high heat 8 minutes or until browned on all sides. Remove beef, reserving drippings in Dutch oven. Add chili powder to Dutch oven; cook, stirring constantly, 1 minute. Stir in tomato paste, and cook, stirring constantly, 2 minutes. Add broth, stirring to loosen particles from bottom of Dutch oven. Return beef to Dutch oven, and stir.

3. Place beef mixture in a 5-qt. slow cooker. Add onion and next 4 ingredients. Cover and cook on LOW 8 hours or until beef is tender. Serve in taco shells with desired toppings.

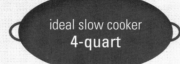

Creamy Beef and Spinach over Noodles

makes 4 to 6 servings • hands-on time: 9 min. • total time: 4 hr., 9 min.

1 lb. ground chuck
1 medium onion, chopped
1 (8-oz.) package sliced fresh
   mushrooms
1 (10-oz.) package frozen chopped
   spinach, thawed
1 (14-oz.) can low-sodium fat-free
   beef broth
1 (10¾-oz.) can cream of mushroom
   soup
1 (8-oz.) container sour cream
½ tsp. salt
¼ tsp. pepper
1 (8-oz.) block Monterey Jack
   cheese with peppers, shredded
Hot cooked egg noodles

1. Cook first 3 ingredients in a large skillet over medium heat, stirring until beef crumbles and is no longer pink; drain.

2. Drain spinach well, pressing between paper towels. Combine beef mixture, spinach, broth, and next 5 ingredients in a large bowl. Spoon into a lightly greased 4-qt. slow cooker. Cover and cook on LOW 4 hours. Serve over egg noodles.

French Dip Sandwiches

Feel free to substitute smaller rolls to make bite-size sandwiches, if desired.

makes 12 servings • hands-on time: 5 min. • total time: 7 hr., 5 min.

1   (3½- to 4-lb.) boneless chuck roast, trimmed and cut in half
½   cup soy sauce
1   beef bouillon cube
1   bay leaf
3   to 4 peppercorns, crushed
1   tsp. dried rosemary, crushed
1   tsp. dried thyme
1   tsp. garlic powder
12 French sandwich rolls, split

1. Place roast in a 5-qt. slow cooker. Combine soy sauce and next 6 ingredients; pour over roast. Add water to slow cooker until roast is almost covered.

2. Cover and cook on LOW 7 hours or until very tender. Remove roast, reserving broth; shred roast with 2 forks. Divide shredded meat evenly among rolls, and serve with reserved broth for dipping.

Beef Brisket with Fall Vegetables

makes 8 servings • hands-on time: 18 min. • total time: 12 hr., 18 min.

2   (2-lb.) beef briskets, trimmed

2   tsp. salt

1   tsp. pepper

1   Tbsp. vegetable oil

4   carrots, peeled and cut into 2-inch pieces

3   parsnips, peeled and sliced

2   celery ribs, sliced

1   large onion, sliced

1   fennel bulb, quartered

12 fresh thyme sprigs

1   (1-oz.) envelope dry onion soup mix

1   (14.5-oz.) can low-sodium beef broth

¾   cup dry red wine

½   cup ketchup

2   Tbsp. Beau Monde seasoning

8   garlic cloves

¾   cup chopped fresh parsley

Garnish: fresh thyme sprigs

1. Sprinkle beef with salt and pepper.

2. Heat oil in a large nonstick skillet over medium-high heat. Add beef; cook 4 minutes on each side or until browned. Transfer beef to a 6-qt. slow cooker. Add carrot and next 5 ingredients.

3. Whisk together soup mix and next 6 ingredients. Pour mixture evenly over beef.

4. Cover and cook on LOW 12 hours or until tender. Transfer beef to a serving platter. Pour remaining vegetable mixture through a wire-mesh strainer, reserving juices, carrot, and onion; discard remaining vegetable mixture. Serve beef and vegetables with juices. Garnish, if desired.

Sloppy Joes

To freeze leftover Sloppy Joe mixture, let cool completely. Place in zip-top plastic freezer bags; lay bags flat, and stack in freezer. Freeze up to one month. Thaw overnight in the fridge, or defrost in the microwave.

makes 8 servings • hands-on time: 14 min. • total time: 4 hr., 14 min.

1½ lb. lean ground beef
1   (16-oz.) package ground pork sausage
1   small onion, chopped
½   medium-size green bell pepper, chopped
1   (8-oz.) can tomato sauce
½   cup ketchup
¼   cup firmly packed brown sugar
2   Tbsp. cider vinegar
2   Tbsp. yellow mustard
1   Tbsp. chili powder
1   Tbsp. Worcestershire sauce
½   tsp. salt
¼   cup all-purpose flour
8   hamburger buns, toasted

1. Brown beef and sausage with onion and bell pepper in a large Dutch oven over medium-high heat, stirring 10 minutes or until beef and sausage crumble and are no longer pink. Drain well.

2. Place beef mixture in a 4-qt. slow cooker. Stir in tomato sauce, ½ cup water, and next 8 ingredients. Cover and cook on HIGH 4 hours. Serve on hamburger buns.

Garlicky Leg of Lamb over Feta Potatoes

makes 8 to 10 servings • hands-on time: 13 min. • total time: 8 hr., 13 min.

1 (4-lb.) boneless leg of lamb, trimmed
8 large garlic cloves
2 tsp. kosher salt
1½ tsp. coarsely ground pepper, divided
2 Tbsp. olive oil
¾ cup red pepper jelly
¼ cup chopped fresh mint
2 Tbsp. balsamic vinegar
2 (24-oz.) packages refrigerated mashed potatoes
6 oz. feta cheese, crumbled
1½ tsp. lemon zest
Garnishes: minced fresh mint, lemon zest

1. Roll up lamb, and tie with string at 2- to 3-inch intervals. Peel and slice garlic cloves in half lengthwise. Cut 16 slits (about ½ inch deep) into lamb; insert a garlic piece into each slit. Rub salt and 1 tsp. pepper all over lamb.

2. Heat oil in a large skillet over medium-high heat. Sear lamb 5 minutes, turning twice with tongs. Place lamb in a lightly greased 5-qt. slow cooker.

3. Combine pepper jelly, next 2 ingredients, and remaining ½ tsp. pepper; stir until jelly is melted. Pour over lamb. Cover and cook on LOW 8 hours or until lamb is very tender.

4. Near the end of cook time, cook 1 package potatoes in microwave according to package directions. Stir potatoes; stir in half of cheese. Cook 3 more minutes. Stir in ¾ tsp. lemon zest. Repeat procedure with remaining potatoes, cheese, and lemon zest.

5. Remove string, and carve lamb; serve with potatoes. Garnish, if desired.

Sweet-and-Spicy
Baby Back Ribs

For smaller appetizer portions, ask the butcher to cut the ribs in half crosswise.

makes 8 servings • hands-on time: 15 min. • total time: 4 hr., 30 min.

2	slabs baby back ribs (about 5 lb.), halved
3	green onions, chopped
1	Tbsp. minced fresh ginger
1½	tsp. jarred minced garlic
1	Tbsp. vegetable oil
1	(12-oz.) bottle chili sauce
1	(8-oz.) bottle hoisin sauce
½	cup applesauce
½	cup beer
2	Tbsp. Worcestershire sauce
1	Tbsp. country-style Dijon mustard
1	to 3 tsp. hot sauce

1. Preheat broiler with oven rack 5½ inches from heat. Place ribs on a lightly greased rack in a lightly greased broiler pan. Broil 10 minutes.

2. Meanwhile, sauté green onion, ginger, and garlic in hot oil in a small saucepan over medium heat 3 to 5 minutes or until tender. Stir in chili sauce and next 6 ingredients. Bring to a boil; reduce heat to medium-low, and simmer 5 minutes.

3. Arrange half of ribs in a single layer in a lightly greased 7-qt. oval slow cooker. Pour half of sauce mixture over ribs. Top with remaining ribs in a single layer. Pour remaining sauce mixture over ribs. Cover and cook on LOW 4 hours or until tender. Transfer to a serving platter.

ideal slow cooker
5-quart

Saucy Chipotle Barbecue Pork

This spicy barbecue pork recipe cooks up an ample amount of sauce—a delicious bonus for barbecue sauce lovers. Use it for dripping over a sandwich, as a dip for fries, or for dressing baked potatoes.

makes 8 servings • hands-on time: 15 min. • total time: 7 hr., 15 min.

2   tsp. dry mustard
1   tsp. salt
½   tsp. ground red pepper
1   (4- to 5-lb.) boneless pork shoulder roast, cut in half (Boston butt)
2   Tbsp. butter
1   large onion, chopped (about 2½ cups)
1   (18-oz.) bottle spicy original barbecue sauce
1   (12-oz.) bottle Baja chipotle marinade
Garnish: sliced green onions

1. Rub first 3 ingredients over pork. Melt butter in a large nonstick skillet over medium-high heat. Add pork; cook 10 minutes or until browned on all sides.

2. Place onion and pork in a 5-qt. slow cooker. Add barbecue sauce, marinade, and ½ cup water.

3. Cover and cook on HIGH 7 hours or until pork is tender and shreds easily.

4. Transfer pork to a large bowl, reserving sauce; shred pork. Stir shredded pork into sauce. Serve as is, over a cheese-topped baked potato, in a sandwich, or over a green salad. Garnish, if desired.

Note: We tested with KC Masterpiece Barbecue Sauce and Lawry's Baja Chipotle Marinade.

Pork Butt Roast

makes 8 to 10 servings • hands-on time: 8 min. • total time: 8 hr., 8 min.

1   (4-lb.) boneless pork shoulder roast (Boston butt)

4   Tbsp. olive oil, divided

2   tsp. salt

2   tsp. pepper

Barbecue sauce (optional)

1. Trim and rinse roast, and pat dry. Rub roast with 1 Tbsp. olive oil. Sprinkle with salt and pepper.

2. Cook roast in remaining 3 Tbsp. hot oil in a large skillet over medium-high heat 2 minutes on each side or until browned. Place roast in a lightly greased 6-qt. slow cooker, fat side up.

3. Cover and cook on HIGH 1 hour. Reduce heat to LOW, and cook 7 hours or until meat is tender and slices easily. Remove pork, reserving liquid; slice meat. Add 1 cup reserved liquid to pork to moisten. Drizzle with barbecue sauce, if desired.

ideal slow cooker
6-quart oval

Honey Mustard-Glazed Ham

makes 8 to 10 servings • hands-on time: 6 min. • total time: 8 hr., 6 min.

1 (7- to 7½-lb.) fully cooked, bone-in ham
¾ cup firmly packed light brown sugar
¾ cup honey
½ cup Dijon mustard
¼ cup apple juice
Garnishes: orange wedges, red grapes, fresh parsley

1. Remove skin and excess fat from ham. Score fat on ham, 1 inch apart, in a diamond pattern. Place ham in a 6-qt. oval slow cooker.

2. Stir together brown sugar and next 3 ingredients in a small bowl. Brush brown sugar mixture over ham. Cover and cook on LOW 8 hours or until a meat thermometer registers 140°. Garnish, if desired.

Slow-Cooker School

We chose the shank portion of the ham because it fits in a slow cooker better and makes a prettier presentation than the butt portion. Examine the ham carefully before purchase to make sure it isn't presliced.

ideal slow cooker
7-quart oval

Ruby Port-Glazed Ham with Dried Fruit Sauce

Stand the ham up on a side so that it fits snugly into the slow cooker.

makes 12 to 14 servings • hands-on time: 11 min. • total time: 6 hr., 26 min.

1   (6½-lb.) fully cooked, bone-in ham (butt portion)
¼   cup stone-ground mustard
1   cup firmly packed light brown sugar
1   cup dried pitted whole dates
1   cup dried pitted plums
½   cup mission figlets, halved
1   cup ruby port or tawny port wine
½   cup fig preserves
Garnish: kumquats

1. Remove skin from ham, and trim fat to ¼-inch thickness. Score fat 1 inch apart in a diamond pattern. Place ham in a 7-qt. oval slow cooker. Brush ham with mustard. Press brown sugar firmly into mustard on ham. Sprinkle dates, plums, and figlets around ham.

2. Stir together port and preserves; drizzle lightly over ham and pour onto fruit. Cover and cook on LOW 6 hours, quickly spooning port mixture over ham twice during cooking.

3. Remove ham from slow cooker, and place on a platter; cover with aluminum foil. Transfer fruit and sauce to a large saucepan. Bring to a boil; boil 15 minutes or until sauce is thickened. Slice ham and spoon sauce over ham. Garnish, if desired.

Cheesy Scalloped Potatoes with Ham

makes 8 servings • hands-on time: 14 min. • total time: 2 hr., 54 min.

6   Tbsp. butter, divided
3   Tbsp. all-purpose flour
2¼   cups evaporated milk
¾   tsp. salt
½   tsp. freshly ground pepper
2   (20-oz.) packages refrigerated
     sliced potatoes
3   cups chopped cooked ham
3   cups (12 oz.) shredded sharp
     Cheddar cheese
1   (3-oz.) package real bacon pieces
¼   cup chopped green onions
Cooking spray

1. Melt 4 Tbsp. butter in a heavy saucepan over low heat; whisk in flour until smooth. Cook 1 minute, whisking constantly. Gradually whisk in milk; cook over medium heat, whisking constantly, until mixture is thickened and bubbly. Stir in salt and pepper.

2. Layer potatoes, milk mixture, ham, and next 3 ingredients in a 5-qt. oval slow cooker coated with cooking spray. Dot with remaining 2 Tbsp. butter.

3. Cover and cook on HIGH 2½ hours or until potatoes are tender. Let stand 10 minutes before serving.

ideal slow cooker
4- or 5-quart

Party Pork and Beans

Shredded smoked barbecue pork flavors these baked beans and makes them the entrée. Serve beans in small ramekins on a picnic plate with the other menu items.

makes 12 servings • hands-on time: 13 min. • total time: 7 hr., 13 min.

4   fully cooked bacon slices
3   (28-oz.) cans baked beans
1   cup refrigerated prechopped
      onion
½   cup firmly packed brown sugar
½   cup barbecue sauce
2   Tbsp. yellow mustard
1   (20-oz.) can pineapple tidbits in
      juice, drained
¾   lb. smoked barbecue pork,
      shredded

1. Prepare bacon according to microwave directions.

2. Meanwhile, stir together beans and next 4 ingredients in a greased 4- or 5-qt. slow cooker. Add 1½ cups pineapple tidbits, reserving remaining tidbits for other uses. Gently stir in pork. Top with bacon slices.

3. Cover and cook on LOW 5 hours. Uncover and cook 2 more hours or until sauce thickens.

Huevos Rancheros

makes 6 servings • hands-on time: 12 min. • total time: 3 hr., 47 min.

1 (1-lb.) package hot ground pork sausage or chorizo sausage

2 cups refrigerated prechopped bell pepper-and-onion mix

1 (28-oz.) can crushed tomatoes

2 (16-oz.) cans pinto beans, drained and rinsed

1½ tsp. ground cumin

1 tsp. dried oregano

10 (6-inch) corn tortillas, divided

6 large eggs

2 cups (8 oz.) shredded pepper Jack or Monterey Jack cheese

Vegetable cooking spray

1 cup pico de gallo or chunky salsa

¼ cup chopped fresh cilantro

2 tsp. chipotle hot sauce

Garnish: fresh cilantro

1. Brown sausage in a large skillet over medium-high heat, stirring until meat crumbles and is no longer pink. Remove sausage from skillet using a slotted spoon; reserve drippings in skillet. Spoon sausage into a 6-qt. oval slow cooker. Sauté bell pepper mix in drippings over medium-high heat 2 minutes. Stir in tomatoes, beans, cumin, and oregano; spoon over sausage in cooker.

2. Meanwhile, tear 4 tortillas into pieces; stir into bean mixture in cooker. Cover and cook on HIGH 3 hours.

3. Make 6 indentations in top of bean mixture in slow cooker, using back of a spoon. Break eggs, one at a time, into a measuring cup; slip eggs, one at a time, into indentations. Cover and cook on HIGH 20 to 30 minutes or until eggs are desired degree of doneness. Uncover and sprinkle with cheese. Turn off cooker; cover and let stand 5 minutes. Preheat oven to 450°. Arrange remaining 6 tortillas on a large baking sheet. Coat both sides with cooking spray. Bake at 450° for 10 to 11 minutes. Stir together pico de gallo, cilantro, and hot sauce.

4. Place tortillas on a platter. Top each tortilla with bean mixture, egg, and pico de gallo mixture. Garnish, if desired.

Sausage-Tomato Cassoulet with Crumb Topping

makes 8 servings • hands-on time: 10 min. • total time: 10 hr., 20 min.

2   lb. mild Italian sausage (about 10 links), cut into ½-inch slices

6   bacon slices, chopped

6   large firm tomatoes, cut into eighths

2   (15½-oz.) cans cannellini beans, drained

2   Tbsp. sugar

1   tsp. dried thyme

½   tsp. salt

½   tsp. freshly ground pepper

1   bay leaf

2   (8-oz.) containers refrigerated prechopped celery, onion, and bell pepper mix

1   Tbsp. jarred minced garlic

2   cups soft, fresh breadcrumbs (about 6 bread slices)

½   cup butter, melted

Garnish: fresh thyme

1. Cook sausage and bacon in a large skillet over medium-high heat 7 minutes or until browned, stirring occasionally.

2. Meanwhile, combine tomatoes and next 6 ingredients in a 6-qt. slow cooker. Remove sausage mixture from skillet with a slotted spoon, reserving 2 tablespoons drippings in skillet. Stir sausage mixture into tomato mixture in slow cooker. Cook celery mix and garlic in hot drippings, stirring often, 3 minutes or until tender.

3. Stir celery mixture into sausage mixture. Cover and cook on LOW 10 hours.

4. Preheat oven to 375°. Place breadcrumbs in a medium bowl; drizzle with melted butter, and toss well. Spread crumb mixture in a single layer on a baking sheet. Bake at 375° for 10 minutes or until browned and crisp. Remove bay leaf, and serve cassoulet hot, topped with toasted crumbs. Garnish, if desired.

Mu Shu Chicken Wraps

makes 8 servings • hands-on time: 11 min. • total time: 6 hr., 11 min.

1	medium onion, diced
2	lb. skinned and boned chicken thighs
¼	tsp. salt
¼	tsp. pepper
1	Tbsp. sesame or vegetable oil
¾	cup hoisin sauce
1	Tbsp. soy sauce
1	Tbsp. honey
2	tsp. rice wine vinegar
¼	tsp. ground ginger
8	(6-inch) flour tortillas
3	cups shredded napa cabbage
½	cup thinly sliced green onions

1. Place onion in a 3- or 4-qt. slow cooker.

2. Sprinkle chicken evenly with salt and pepper.

3. Brown chicken 2 to 3 minutes on each side in hot oil in a large skillet over medium-high heat. Remove skillet from heat, and place chicken on top of onion in slow cooker.

4. Whisk together hoisin sauce and next 4 ingredients; pour over chicken. Cover and cook on HIGH 1 hour. Reduce heat to LOW, and cook 5 hours. Shred chicken in cooker with fork.

5. Top each tortilla with cabbage, chicken, and green onions; roll up. If desired, secure with string.

ideal slow cooker
4-quart

Shredded Barbecue Chicken

makes 6 servings • hands-on time: 22 min. • total time: 7 hr., 22 min.

1½ lb. skinned and boned chicken thighs
1 Tbsp. olive oil
1 cup ketchup
¼ cup dark brown sugar
1 Tbsp. Worcestershire sauce
1 Tbsp. cider vinegar
1 Tbsp. yellow mustard
1 tsp. ground red pepper
½ tsp. garlic salt
6 hamburger buns
Dill pickle slices

1. Brown chicken 4 minutes on each side in hot oil in a large skillet over medium-high heat. Remove from heat, and place in a 4-qt. slow cooker.

2. Combine ketchup and next 6 ingredients. Pour over chicken.

3. Cover and cook on HIGH 1 hour. Reduce heat to LOW and cook 5 to 6 hours. Remove chicken from sauce; shred chicken. Stir shredded chicken back into sauce. Spoon mixture onto buns, and top with pickle slices.

Chicken, Broccoli, Bacon, and Rice

makes 8 servings • hands-on time: 16 min. • total time: 7 hr., 16 min.

1   slow-cooker liner

Cooking spray

1½ cups instant white rice

6   skinned and boned chicken breasts

1   tsp. salt

½   tsp. pepper

1   cup matchstick carrots

2   cups (8 oz.) shredded sharp Cheddar cheese, divided

1   cup frozen prechopped onion

1   (8-oz.) can sliced water chestnuts, drained

2   (10¾-oz.) cans cream of chicken soup

6   fully cooked bacon slices

1   (16-oz.) package frozen broccoli cuts (do not thaw)

2   to 3 cups coarsely crushed ridged potato chips

1. Place slow cooker liner in a 5- or 6-qt. slow cooker. Coat liner with cooking spray. Place rice in liner. Sprinkle chicken with salt and pepper. Heat a large nonstick skillet over medium-high heat. Coat pan with cooking spray. Sauté chicken, in 2 batches, 2 minutes on each side or until browned. Place on top of rice. Top with carrots, 1 cup cheese, onion, and water chestnuts. Sprinkle with remaining 1 cup cheese. Top with soup. Pour 1½ cups water around edges.

2. Cover and cook on LOW 6 hours, stirring gently after 5 hours to break chicken into chunks. Coarsely crumble bacon; add to slow cooker. Stir in broccoli. Cover and cook on LOW 1 more hour. Top with chips before serving.

Slow-Cooker School

Chicken breaks apart easily after 5 or more hours of slow cooking on LOW. Stir gently, breaking up chicken with a spoon as you stir.

Chicken Chow Mein

makes 6 to 8 servings • hands-on time: 10 min. • total time: 3 hr., 10 min.

1 red bell pepper, cut into strips
2 lb. chicken breast tenders or
  2 lb. skinned and boned chicken
  breasts, cut into strips
½ tsp. pepper
1 Tbsp. vegetable oil
½ cup lite soy sauce
¼ cup oyster sauce
1 Tbsp. dark sesame oil
2 tsp. grated fresh ginger
1 Tbsp. cornstarch
2 cups frozen broccoli cuts
  (do not thaw)
1 cup fully cooked, shelled frozen
  edamame (green soybeans)
  (do not thaw)
2 (8-oz.) cans sliced water chestnuts,
  drained
Hot cooked rice
3 green onions, diagonally sliced
1 (3-oz.) can chow mein noodles
  (optional)

1. Place bell pepper strips in a lightly greased 4- or 5-qt. slow cooker. Sprinkle chicken with pepper. Heat oil in a large nonstick skillet over medium-high heat. Sauté chicken 2 minutes on each side; transfer to slow cooker.

2. Combine soy sauce and next 3 ingredients; pour over chicken in slow cooker. Cover and cook on LOW 2 hours.

3. Combine cornstarch and 2 Tbsp. water, stirring until smooth. Stir into mixture in slow cooker. Stir in broccoli, edamame, and water chestnuts. Cover and cook on LOW 1 hour.

4. Serve over rice. Sprinkle with green onions. Top with chow mein noodles, if desired.

Rosemary Chicken Lasagna

makes 8 to 10 servings • hands-on time: 13 min. • total time: 3 hr., 13 min.

2   Tbsp. olive oil

1½   to 2 Tbsp. chopped fresh rosemary

1   Tbsp. jarred minced garlic

1   cup frozen prechopped onion

4   cups chopped cooked chicken

Freshly ground pepper to taste

2   (15-oz.) jars Alfredo sauce

1   (9-oz.) box no-boil lasagna noodles

1   (15-oz.) container ricotta cheese

1   (8-oz.) container sour cream

1   large egg, lightly beaten

½   tsp. freshly ground pepper

4   cups (16 oz.) shredded mozzarella
     cheese

½   cup coarsely chopped pitted
     kalamata olives

Garnish: fresh rosemary

1. Heat oil in a large skillet over medium-high heat. Sauté rosemary and garlic in hot oil 1 minute or until very fragrant. Add onion; sauté 4 to 5 minutes or until browned. Remove from heat; stir in chicken. Sprinkle with desired amount of pepper.

2. Spread 1 cup Alfredo sauce in bottom of a lightly greased 5-qt. oval slow cooker. Arrange 6 uncooked noodles over sauce, breaking noodles as needed to fit in slow cooker. Top with one-third of chicken mixture.

3. Combine ricotta cheese and next 3 ingredients in a bowl. Spread 1 cup ricotta mixture over chicken mixture. Sprinkle with 1 cup mozzarella. Repeat layers twice with 1 cup Alfredo sauce, 5 uncooked noodles, half each of remaining chicken mixture, remaining ricotta mixture, and remaining mozzarella.

4. Cover and cook on LOW 3 hours. Top with olives before serving. Garnish, if desired.

Chicken Tetrazzini

makes 8 to 10 servings • hands-on time: 15 min. • total time: 4 hr., 25 min.

8   Tbsp. butter, divided
1   (8-oz.) package sliced fresh
     mushrooms
1   onion, chopped
½   cup all-purpose flour
4   cups milk
¼   cup Marsala
½   tsp. salt
½   tsp. freshly ground pepper
12   oz. uncooked spaghetti, broken
     in half
4   cups chopped cooked chicken
½   cup (8 oz.) slivered almonds,
     toasted
2   cups freshly grated Parmigiano-
     Reggiano cheese

1. Melt 2 Tbsp. butter in a large deep skillet over medium-high heat. Add mushrooms and onion; sauté 3 to 4 minutes or until tender. Remove mushroom mixture, and set aside.

2. Melt remaining 6 Tbsp. butter in skillet; whisk in flour until smooth. Cook 1 minute, whisking constantly. Gradually whisk in milk; bring to a boil. Cook 2 to 3 minutes or until mixture thickens, stirring constantly. Stir in Marsala, salt, and pepper.

3. Spoon one-third of milk mixture into a 5- or 6-qt. slow cooker. Top with half of spaghetti, half of mushroom mixture, half of chicken, half of almonds, and half of cheese. Repeat layers with one-third of milk mixture, and remaining spaghetti, mushroom mixture, chicken, and almonds. Top with remaining milk mixture; sprinkle with remaining cheese. Cover and cook on LOW 4 hours. Let stand 10 minutes before serving.

Open-Faced Sloppy Toms

makes 6 to 8 servings • hands-on time: 12 min. • total time: 6 hr., 12 min.

2   lb. ground turkey

2   (8-oz.) packages frozen chopped celery, onion, and bell pepper mix

1   Tbsp. jarred minced garlic

1   (15-oz.) can tomato sauce

1   (6-oz.) can tomato paste

⅓   cup firmly packed light brown sugar

¼   cup cider vinegar

2   Tbsp. Worcestershire sauce

2   tsp. paprika

½   tsp. chili powder

½   tsp. salt

½   tsp. freshly ground pepper

6   to 8 slices Texas toast

Garnishes: finely chopped red onion, dill pickle slices

1. Brown first three ingredients in a large skillet over medium-high heat, stirring often, 10 minutes or until turkey crumbles and is no longer pink.

2. Meanwhile, combine tomato sauce and next 8 ingredients in a 5-qt. slow cooker. Stir turkey mixture into tomato sauce mixture. Cover and cook on LOW 6 hours.

3. Prepare Texas toast according to package directions. To serve, spoon turkey mixture over toast. Garnish, if desired.

Mediterranean Roast Turkey

makes 8 servings • hands-on time: 13 min. • total time: 7 hr., 43 min.

1   Tbsp. olive oil

1   (4-lb.) boneless turkey breast, trimmed

2   cups chopped onion

½   cup pitted kalamata olives

½   cup julienne-cut oil-packed sun-dried tomato halves, drained

2   Tbsp. fresh lemon juice

1½   tsp. jarred minced garlic

1   tsp. Greek seasoning mix

½   tsp. salt

¼   tsp. freshly ground pepper

½   cup chicken broth, divided

3   Tbsp. all-purpose flour

1. Heat olive oil in a large skillet over medium-high heat. Add turkey breast to skillet, and brown on all sides, about 8 minutes.

2. Combine turkey, onion, and next 7 ingredients in a 6-qt. slow cooker. Add ¼ cup chicken broth. Cover and cook on LOW 7 hours.

3. Combine remaining ¼ cup broth and flour in a small bowl; stir with a whisk until smooth. Add broth mixture to slow cooker. Cover and cook on LOW 30 minutes. Cut turkey into slices; serve with gravy.

ideal slow cooker
6- or 7-quart

Bouillabaisse

Halibut, grouper, and snapper are good fish choices for this recipe. Choose pieces that are about an inch thick.

makes 6 to 8 servings • hands-on time: 9 min. • total time: 3 hr., 9 min.

1   small fennel bulb, thinly sliced

1   (8-oz.) container refrigerated prechopped celery, onion, and bell pepper mix

1   Tbsp. olive oil

2   (14½-oz.) cans diced tomatoes with basil, garlic, and oregano, undrained

1   bay leaf

1   (8-oz.) bottle clam juice

1   cup dry white wine

½   tsp. salt

½   tsp. freshly ground pepper

3   lb. whitefish pieces

1½ lb. fresh mussels, scrubbed and debearded

1   lb. unpeeled, large raw shrimp

Garnishes: lemon wedges, chopped fresh parsley

1. Sauté fennel and celery mix in hot oil in a large skillet over medium-high heat 3 to 4 minutes or until tender. Stir in tomatoes and bay leaf. Pour mixture into a lightly greased 6- or 7-qt. slow cooker. Stir in clam juice and next 3 ingredients. Cover and cook on HIGH 2 hours or until simmering.

2. Stir fish, mussels, and shrimp into broth mixture in slow cooker. Reduce heat to LOW. Cover and cook on LOW 1 hour or until seafood is done. Discard bay leaf. Spoon stew into large shallow bowls. Garnish, if desired.

ideal slow cooker
5-quart

Easy Jambalaya

makes 8 servings • hands-on time: 11 min. • total time: 5 hr., 41 min.

2   lb. skinned and boned chicken thighs

1   lb. smoked sausage, cut into 2-inch slices

1   (8-oz.) container refrigerated prechopped celery, onion, and bell pepper mix

1   (28-oz.) can diced tomatoes, undrained

3   garlic cloves, chopped

2   cups chicken broth

1   Tbsp. Cajun spice mix

1   tsp. dried thyme

1   tsp. dried oregano

¾   lb. peeled, extra-large raw shrimp

1¾ cups converted rice

Garnish: chopped parsley

1. Combine chicken, sausage, and next 7 ingredients in a 5-qt. slow cooker. Cover and cook on LOW 5 hours.

2. Add shrimp and rice, and increase heat to HIGH. Cover and cook 30 minutes. Garnish, if desired.

How to Peel & Devein Shrimp

It's fastest to purchase shrimp that has already been peeled and deveined, but if you'd like to start with shrimp in the shell, begin by peeling the  shrimp. Then cut a shallow slit along the back of the shrimp using a sharp paring knife. Lift and remove the dark vein with the knife tip. Rinse shrimp under cold water; drain. One pound of shrimp in the shell equals ¾ pound of peeled and deveined shrimp.

Paella

makes 8 servings   •   hands-on time: 15 min.   •   total time: 2 hr., 30 min.

3   (5-oz.) packages yellow rice
1   lb. chorizo sausage, cut diagonally into ½-inch slices
3   cups pulled deli-roasted chicken
1   (8-oz.) container refrigerated prechopped tricolor bell pepper
1   (5¾-oz.) jar pimiento-stuffed Spanish olives, drained
1   (8-oz.) container refrigerated prechopped onion
1   tsp. jarred minced garlic
1   (14½-oz.) can diced tomatoes, undrained
¾   lb. unpeeled, medium-size raw shrimp
1   cup frozen English peas

1. Place rice in bottom of a lightly greased 5-qt. slow cooker. Sauté chorizo in a large skillet over medium-high heat 4 minutes or until browned. Remove sausage from skillet with a slotted spoon, reserving 2 Tbsp. drippings in pan. Layer sausage, chicken, and next 2 ingredients over rice.

2. Sauté onion and garlic in hot drippings 3 minutes or until lightly browned. Add 4 cups water and tomatoes, stirring to loosen particles from bottom of skillet. Bring to a boil; remove from heat. Pour onion mixture over chicken mixture in slow cooker. (Do not stir.) Cover and cook on LOW 2 hours.

3. Meanwhile, peel and devein shrimp, leaving tails intact.

4. Increase heat to HIGH. Add shrimp and peas to slow cooker. Cover and cook 15 minutes or until shrimp turn pink.

Secret Ingredient

Mexican chorizo is made with fresh pork, while Spanish chorizo is made with smoked pork. Because of this, the Mexican chorizo is ideal to use for home cooking. It can be eaten as is, but is often used as a replacement for ground pork or beef in a recipe.

ideal slow cooker
4½-quart

Holiday Gingerbread Pudding

makes 8 to 10 servings • hands-on time: 21 minutes • total time: 5 hr., 6 min.

1 (12-oz.) French bread loaf, cut into
   1-inch cubes

1½ cups chopped pecans, toasted

1 cup raisins

3 large eggs, lightly beaten

3 cups half-and-half

1 cup firmly packed light brown
   sugar

¾ cup molasses

¼ cup butter, melted

1 Tbsp. vanilla extract

2 tsp. ground cinnamon

½ tsp. salt

½ tsp. ground ginger

½ tsp. ground nutmeg

Spiced Whipped Cream

1. Combine first 3 ingredients in a 4½-qt. slow cooker. Whisk together eggs and next 9 ingredients in a medium bowl. Pour over bread mixture, stirring well to coat; cover and let stand 30 minutes. Stir again to coat bread evenly with egg mixture.

2. Cover and cook on LOW 4 hours or until set. Let stand 15 minutes before serving. Serve with Spiced Whipped Cream.

Spiced Whipped Cream

makes 2 cups • hands-on time: 5 minutes • total time: 5 min.

1 cup whipping cream

3 Tbsp. brown sugar

1 Tbsp. pecan liqueur (optional)

1. Beat whipping cream, sugar, and, if desired, liqueur at medium speed with an electric mixer until stiff peaks form.

Cranberry-Apple Cobbler

makes 6 to 8 servings • hands-on time: 21 min. • total time: 4 hr., 21 min.

5	Granny Smith apples, peeled and sliced (about 3 lb.)
2	cups fresh or frozen cranberries
1	cup firmly packed light brown sugar
1	tsp. vanilla extract
1	tsp. ground cinnamon
2	tsp. cornstarch
1	vanilla bean, split
1	cup all-purpose flour
¾	tsp. baking powder
⅛	tsp. salt
⅓	cup butter, softened
⅓	cup granulated sugar
1	Tbsp. milk
1	large egg
Vanilla ice cream	

1. Combine first 5 ingredients in a lightly greased 5-qt. slow cooker.

2. Whisk together cornstarch and ¼ cup water until smooth; add to slow cooker, stirring well.

3. Cover and cook on HIGH 1½ hours.

4. Meanwhile, use a small, sharp knife to scrape seeds from vanilla bean, discarding pod. Combine vanilla seeds and next 3 ingredients; set aside.

5. Beat butter at medium speed with an electric mixer until creamy. Gradually add granulated sugar, beating well; add milk and egg, beating until blended. Stir in flour mixture.

6. Stir apple mixture. Drop flour mixture, 1 Tbsp. at a time, over apple mixture.

7. Reduce heat to LOW; cover and cook 2½ hours. Serve warm with ice cream.

Baked Four-Cheese Spaghetti
with Italian Sausage, page 228

Weeknight Favorites

Butternut Squash Soup with Vanilla Bean

makes 6 servings • hands-on time: 8 min. • total time: 6 hr., 28 min.

3 (11-oz.) containers refrigerated cubed peeled butternut squash (6 cups), chopped

1 cup refrigerated prechopped onion

1 Braeburn apple, peeled and coarsely chopped

1½ cups apple cider

1 cup chicken broth

1 vanilla bean, split lengthwise

1 rosemary sprig

½ cup whipping cream

¼ tsp. salt

Garnishes: fresh rosemary, additional whipping cream

1. Stir together first 5 ingredients in a 5-qt. slow cooker. Scrape vanilla bean seeds into slow cooker; add vanilla bean pod and rosemary sprig. Stir well. Cover and cook on LOW 6 hours or until squash is very tender. Uncover and cool 20 minutes. Discard vanilla bean and rosemary.

2. Process mixture with a handheld blender (immersion blender) until smooth. Stir in whipping cream and salt. Garnish, if desired.

How to Peel & Cube Butternut Squash

If you prefer to peel and cube your own, look for butternut squash that has no cracks or soft spots.

1. Cut the squash in half, and remove the seeds and fibers with a spoon or your fingers.

2. Holding one half of the squash in your hand, use a vegetable peeler to remove the skin. Cut the squash into cubes.

Roasted Mushroom Soup with Sourdough Croutons

makes 6 to 8 servings • hands-on time: 15 min. • total time: 3 hr., 30 min.

4 (4-oz.) packages sliced fresh gourmet mushroom blend

2 (8-oz.) packages sliced fresh mushrooms

4 Tbsp. olive oil, divided

1 tsp. kosher salt

½ tsp. freshly ground pepper

2 (8-oz.) containers refrigerated prechopped celery, onion, and bell pepper mix

1 Tbsp. jarred minced garlic

1 cup dry white wine

2 cups vegetable broth

½ tsp. ground sage

¼ tsp. ground nutmeg

1 cup heavy cream

¼ cup all-purpose flour

4 (1-inch-thick) sourdough bread slices, cut into 1-inch cubes

Garnish: chopped fresh chives

1. Preheat broiler with oven rack 5½ inches from heat. Spread mushrooms in a single layer on an aluminum foil-lined rimmed baking sheet. Drizzle with 2 Tbsp. olive oil; sprinkle with salt and pepper. Broil 12 minutes or until browned. Heat 1 Tbsp. oil in a skillet over medium-high heat. Add celery mix and garlic; sauté 3 minutes. Stir in wine, and cook 5 minutes or until liquid is reduced by half.

2. Combine mushrooms and juices, celery mixture, broth, and next 2 ingredients in a 5-qt. slow cooker. Cover and cook on HIGH 3 hours. Stir cream into soup. Stir together flour and ¼ cup water until smooth. Stir into soup. Cover and cook 15 more minutes or until thickened. During last 30 minutes of cook time, preheat oven to 350°. Toss bread cubes with remaining 1 Tbsp. oil. Place on a baking sheet. Bake at 350° for 10 minutes. Serve croutons with soup. Garnish, if desired.

Beer-Braised Pork and Black Bean Soup

makes 6 servings • hands-on time: 11 min. • total time: 8 hr., 11 min.

1½ lb. boneless pork shoulder roast (Boston butt)
2   Tbsp. olive oil
2   (12-oz.) bottles beer
1   Tbsp. chopped canned chipotle peppers in adobo sauce
1   Tbsp. adobo sauce from can
1   tsp. ground cumin
1   large onion, chopped
1   lb. dried black beans, rinsed
1½ tsp. kosher salt
½   cup sour cream
½   cup store-bought refrigerated fresh salsa
¼   cup chopped fresh cilantro

1. Cook pork in hot oil in a Dutch oven over medium-high heat 3 minutes on each side or until browned on all sides.

2. Combine beer, 3 cups water, peppers, adobo sauce, cumin, onion, beans, salt, and pork in a 6-qt. slow cooker. Cover and cook on LOW 8 hours. Using 2 forks, separate pork into large pieces. Divide among individual bowls, and top with sour cream, salsa, and cilantro.

Peppered Beef Soup

makes 6 servings • hands-on time: 13 min. • total time: 8 hr., 13 min.

1	(4-lb.) sirloin tip beef roast
½	cup all-purpose flour
2	Tbsp. canola oil
1	cup refrigerated prechopped red onion
2	tsp. jarred minced garlic
2	large baking potatoes, peeled and diced
1	(16-oz.) package baby carrots
2	(12-oz.) bottles lager beer
2	Tbsp. balsamic vinegar
2	Tbsp. Worcestershire sauce
2	Tbsp. dried parsley flakes
1	Tbsp. beef bouillon granules
1½	to 3 tsp. freshly ground pepper
4	bay leaves
½	tsp. salt

1. Rinse roast, and pat dry. Cut a 1-inch-deep cavity in the shape of an "X" on top of roast. (Do not cut all the way through roast.) Dredge roast in flour; shake off excess.

2. Cook roast in hot oil in a Dutch oven over medium-high heat 1 to 2 minutes on each side or until lightly browned.

3. Place roast in a 6-qt. slow cooker. Stuff cavity with red onion and garlic; top roast with potatoes and carrots. Pour beer, vinegar, and Worcestershire sauce into slow cooker. Sprinkle with parsley, bouillon, and pepper. Add bay leaves to liquid in slow cooker.

4. Cover and cook on LOW 7 to 8 hours or until fork-tender. Shred roast using 2 forks. Season with salt. Discard bay leaves.

Note: 3 cups low-sodium beef broth may be substituted for the beer.

Spicy Chicken Stew

If you know that you will be using chopped vegetables in meals like this one several times during the week, chop them all at once, and store them in the refrigerator in zip-top plastic bags.

makes 6 servings • hands-on time: 15 min. • total time: 6 hr., 15 min.

2   skinned and boned chicken breasts (about 1 lb.)

4   skinned and boned chicken thighs (about 10½ oz.)

1   Tbsp. olive oil

2   baking potatoes (about 1½ lb.), peeled and cut into chunks (3⅓ cups)

2   cups frozen sweet corn

2   celery ribs, chopped

2   carrots, peeled and cut into chunks (1 cup)

1   onion, thickly sliced

1   tsp. jarred minced garlic

1   (12.5-oz.) jar salsa

2   tsp. kosher salt

1½   tsp. ground cumin

1   tsp. chili powder

½   tsp. pepper

2½   cups chicken broth

4   (6-inch) corn tortillas, cut into strips

1. Cook chicken in hot oil in a Dutch oven over medium-high heat 3 minutes on each side or until browned.

2. Place potatoes and next 5 ingredients in a 5-qt. slow cooker. Stir in salsa and next 4 ingredients. Place chicken on top of vegetables, and pour chicken broth over chicken. Cover and cook on LOW 6 hours.

3. Transfer chicken to a plate, and shred with 2 forks into bite-size chunks; return to slow cooker. Spoon stew into bowls. Top with tortilla strips.

ideal slow cooker
4- or 5-quart

Chicken Sausage and White Bean Stew

Fire-roasted tomatoes are a new product on grocery shelves. These canned tomatoes have been roasted over an open fire to produce a subtle, smoky, grilled flavor—ideal for stews like this one.

makes 4 servings • hands-on time: 11 min. • total time: 8 hr., 11 min.

1   (12-oz.) package spinach-and-
    feta chicken sausage, sliced
3   carrots, coarsely chopped
1   medium onion, chopped
½   tsp. salt
½   tsp. dried rosemary
¼   tsp. pepper
1   (14½-oz.) can fire-roasted diced
    tomatoes
2   (15.8-oz.) cans great Northern
    beans, undrained
4   bacon slices, cooked and crumbled

1. Cook sausage in a large skillet over medium-high heat 4 minutes or until browned.

2. Place carrot and onion in a 4- or 5-qt. slow cooker; sprinkle with salt, rosemary, and pepper. Layer tomatoes and beans over carrot mixture. Top with sausage. Cover and cook on LOW 8 hours or until vegetables are tender. Sprinkle with bacon before serving.

Irish Lamb Stew

makes 8 to 10 servings   •   hands-on time: 13 min.   •   total time: 7 hr., 33 min.

3   center-cut bacon slices
2   lb. boneless lean lamb, cut into
½-inch pieces
1   tsp. salt
½   tsp. freshly ground pepper
¾   cup (¼-inch-thick) carrot slices
½   cup diced celery
3   garlic cloves, minced
2   (14-oz.) cans beef broth
1   lb. small round red potatoes,
quartered
1   small onion, cut into thin wedges
¼   cup cornstarch
Chopped fresh marjoram

1. Cook bacon in a large skillet over medium-high heat 4 to 5 minutes or until crisp; remove bacon, and drain on paper towels, reserving drippings in skillet. Coarsely crumble bacon.

2. Sprinkle lamb with salt and pepper; add to drippings in skillet. Cook lamb 5 minutes or until browned on all sides, stirring occasionally. Stir in 2 cups water, stirring to loosen particles from bottom of skillet. Transfer lamb mixture to a 5-qt. slow cooker. Stir in crumbled bacon, carrot, and next 5 ingredients. Cover and cook on LOW 7 hours or until lamb is tender.

3. Increase slow cooker temperature to HIGH. Combine cornstarch and 3 Tbsp. water in a small bowl, stirring until smooth. Stir cornstarch mixture into stew. Cover and cook 20 minutes or until slightly thickened, stirring occasionally. Ladle stew into bowls; sprinkle with marjoram.

Make it *Easier*

If available, purchase lamb stew meat. This will save trimming and cutting time.

ideal slow cooker
5- or 6-quart

Game-Day Chili

makes 8 servings • hands-on time: 14 min. • total time: 4 hr., 14 min.

3¼ lb. ground chuck

1 medium-size green bell pepper, chopped

3 (14½-oz.) cans diced tomatoes with garlic and onion, undrained

3 (10¾-oz.) cans tomato soup

1 (16-oz.) can light red kidney beans, drained and rinsed

1 (6-oz.) can tomato paste

5 Tbsp. chili powder

1 tsp. freshly ground pepper

½ tsp. paprika

Toppings: sour cream, shredded Cheddar cheese, chopped green onions, sliced black olives, corn chips

1. Cook meat in a large nonstick skillet over medium-high heat 12 to 14 minutes or until meat crumbles and is no longer pink; drain.

2. Place meat in a 5- or 6-qt. slow cooker; stir in ½ cup water, bell pepper, and next 7 ingredients. Cover and cook on HIGH 4 hours. Serve with desired toppings.

Make it *Easier*

Freeze any leftovers for a great make-ahead cold-weather comfort dish. Omit the beans, if desired.

Cincinnati 5-Way Chili

This chili originated with Greek immigrant restaurateurs, who began serving chili over spaghetti.

makes 4 servings • hands-on time: 13 min. • total time: 6 hr., 13 min.

1½ lb. ground sirloin
1   large onion, chopped
2   garlic cloves, minced
Cooking spray
2   Tbsp. chili powder
1½ Tbsp. unsweetened cocoa
1   Tbsp. cider vinegar
1   Tbsp. Worcestershire sauce
1   tsp. ground allspice
1   tsp. ground cinnamon
½   tsp. salt
¼   tsp. ground red pepper
1   bay leaf
1   (12-oz.) bottle German beer
1   (6-oz.) can tomato paste
Hot cooked spaghetti
Toppings: shredded sharp Cheddar
         cheese, diced onion, and
         1 (15-oz.) can kidney beans,
         drained and rinsed

1. Cook beef, chopped onion, and garlic in a large nonstick skillet coated with cooking spray over medium-high heat 8 minutes or until browned. Stir in chili powder, next 10 ingredients, and ½ cup water. Transfer chili mixture to a 4- or 5-qt. slow cooker. Cover and cook on LOW 6 hours. Discard bay leaf.

2. Serve chili over hot cooked spaghetti. Top with cheese, diced onion, and kidney beans.

Tomatillo-Mushroom Chili

makes 8 servings • hands-on time: 17 min. • total time: 3 hr., 17 min.

1 Tbsp. extra virgin olive oil
6 tomatillos, husks removed, coarsely chopped
2 onions, coarsely chopped
2 garlic cloves, minced
1 lb. shiitake mushrooms, stems removed, coarsely chopped
2 Tbsp. chili powder
1 tsp. ground cumin
3 cups organic vegetable broth
2 (15-oz.) cans black beans, drained and rinsed
1 (14½-oz.) can fire-roasted diced tomatoes, undrained
Garnishes: shredded Cheddar cheese, chopped green onions

1. Heat a large skillet over medium-high heat; add oil. Sauté tomatillos, onions, and garlic in hot oil 7 minutes or until tender. Add mushrooms, chili powder, and cumin; sauté 3 minutes.

2. Transfer vegetable mixture to a 5-qt. slow cooker; stir in broth and next 2 ingredients. Cover and cook on LOW 3 hours. Garnish, if desired.

Secret Ingredient

A slightly tarter cousin of tomatoes and a bit meatier, tomatillos are about the size of a cherry tomato and grow inside a papery husk. Store this staple of Mexican cooking in a paper bag in the refrigerator for up to one month. Do not store them in an airtight container. They may also be frozen either whole or sliced.

Seafood Gumbo

makes 6 servings • hands-on time: 20 min. • total time: 3 hr., 20 min.

½   lb. sliced bacon, diced

2   (8-oz.) containers refrigerated prechopped celery, onion, and green pepper mix

2   garlic cloves, minced

2   cups chicken broth

1   (14-oz.) can diced tomatoes

2   Tbsp. Worcestershire sauce

2   tsp. kosher salt

1   tsp. dried thyme leaves

¾   lb. peeled, large raw shrimp

1   lb. fresh or frozen crabmeat

2   cups frozen cut okra

Hot cooked rice

1. Cook bacon in a large skillet over medium heat until crisp. With a slotted spoon, transfer bacon to a 5-qt. slow cooker. Discard all but a thin coating of drippings in skillet. Add celery mix and garlic to skillet, and cook over medium heat, stirring frequently, until vegetables are tender, about 10 minutes.

2. Spoon vegetables into slow cooker; add broth, tomatoes, Worcestershire, salt, and thyme. Cover and cook on HIGH 2 hours.

3. Reduce temperature to LOW. Add shrimp, crabmeat, and okra, and cook on LOW 1 hour. Serve over hot cooked rice.

Slow-Cooker School

This recipe skips the tedious steps and hard-to-find spices of traditional gumbos without compromising any of the flavor.

Cranberry Corned Beef

makes 6 to 8 servings • hands-on time: 12 min. • total time: 9 hr., 12 min.

1 (4-lb.) cured corned beef brisket with spice packet
5 large carrots, cut into 3-inch pieces
1 large onion, cut into 6 wedges
1 (14-oz.) can whole-berry cranberry sauce
1 (14-oz.) can jellied cranberry sauce
2 (1-oz.) envelopes dry onion soup mix
½ cup sour cream
4 tsp. refrigerated horseradish
¼ tsp. freshly ground pepper
Garnish: chopped fresh parsley

1. Trim fat from brisket. Place carrots and onion in a 5-qt. slow cooker; place brisket on top of vegetables. Sprinkle spice packet over brisket.

2. Combine cranberry sauces and soup mix. Spoon over brisket. Cover and cook on HIGH 1 hour. Reduce heat to LOW, and cook 8 hours.

3. Meanwhile, combine sour cream and horseradish in a small bowl. Cover and chill until ready to serve.

4. Transfer brisket to a serving platter. Spoon carrot, onion, and, if desired, a little cooking liquid around brisket on platter. Serve with sauce. Sprinkle with pepper. Garnish, if desired.

Slow-Cooker School

The long, slow cooking process makes corned beef an ideal meat for the slow cooker. The meat does tend to shrink in the slow cooker, so cooking a large portion such as this works well.

ideal slow cooker
5-quart

Spicy Shredded Beef Sandwiches

Save extra sauce to use as a topping for Mexican rice or cooked pinto beans.

makes 6 to 8 servings • hands-on time: 5 min. • total time: 9 hr., 5 min.

1 (2½-lb.) boneless chuck roast, trimmed

1 (14½-oz.) can diced tomatoes, undrained

1 (7-oz.) can adobo sauce or 1 (7-oz.) jar spicy salsa

1 (4-oz.) can jalapeño peppers, drained

1 (8-oz.) container refrigerated prechopped onion (about 1¾ cups)

1½ tsp. jarred minced garlic

2 Tbsp. chili powder

1 Tbsp. honey

2½ tsp. kosher salt

1 tsp. ground cumin

2 cups beef broth

Crusty French rolls

Toppings: shredded cabbage, sliced red onion, sliced tomato, sour cream, chopped cilantro

1. Place beef in a 5-qt. slow cooker. Add tomatoes, and next 8 ingredients; pour broth over beef.

2. Cover and cook on HIGH 1 hour; reduce heat to LOW, and cook 8 hours. If desired, remove lid during last 30 minutes to allow sauce to reduce and thicken.

3. With a heavy fork, transfer meat to a rimmed cutting board or plate. Shred with 2 forks. Ladle out half the sauce and reserve for another use. Return shredded beef to the remaining sauce in slow cooker; keep warm. Serve on rolls. Add desired toppings.

Beef Stroganoff

Look for beef sirloin tips as a time-saver. Or purchase top sirloin, and thinly slice.

makes 6 to 8 servings • hands-on time: 15 min. • total time: 3 hr., 15 min.

¼ cup all-purpose flour
2 lb. beef sirloin tips
½ tsp. salt
½ tsp. freshly ground pepper
2 Tbsp. olive oil
2 medium onions, chopped
2 (8-oz.) packages sliced fresh
    mushrooms
1½ cups beef broth
2 Tbsp. tomato paste
1 Tbsp. Dijon mustard
1½ cups sour cream
¼ cup dry sherry (optional)
Hot cooked egg noodles
Chopped fresh parsley (optional)

1. Place flour in a shallow dish. Sprinkle beef with salt and pepper; dredge in flour. Heat a large skillet over medium-high heat; add oil. Add beef; cook 7 minutes or until browned, stirring occasionally. Transfer to a greased 5-qt. slow cooker. Add onion and mushrooms to drippings in skillet; cook, stirring often, 3 minutes or until tender.

2. Meanwhile, combine broth, tomato paste, and mustard. Add broth mixture to skillet, stirring to loosen particles from bottom of skillet. Pour over beef in slow cooker.

3. Cover and cook on LOW 3 hours or until beef is tender. Just before serving, stir in sour cream and, if desired, sherry. Serve over noodles. Sprinkle with parsley, if desired.

Beef Ragu with Penne

You can substitute gemelli, cellentani, or macaroni for the penne.

makes 4 servings • hands-on time: 8 min. • total time: 4 hr., 8 min.

1   large onion, chopped

2   lb. ground beef

2   (28-oz.) cans crushed tomatoes

1   tsp. kosher salt

1   (16-oz.) package penne pasta

¼   cup finely grated Parmesan cheese

2   Tbsp. chopped fresh basil

Freshly ground pepper to taste

1. Place onion in a 5-qt. slow cooker. Crumble ground beef over onion, and add tomatoes. Cover and cook on HIGH 4 hours or on LOW 8 hours. Break up any large pieces of beef with a wooden spoon. Add salt. Remove half of sauce, and reserve for another use; keep remaining sauce warm in slow cooker.

2. Cook pasta according to package directions, stirring often. Drain and transfer to 4 shallow bowls. Spoon meat sauce over each portion of pasta. Serve with Parmesan cheese, basil, and pepper.

ideal slow cooker
5-quart

Pappardelle Bolognese

Pappardelle is pasta shaped like wide ribbons. If your store doesn't stock it, you may substitute the more narrow fettuccine, or, narrower still, tagliatelle.

makes 6 servings • hands-on time: 15 min. • total time: 6 hr., 15 min.

2   Tbsp. olive oil
2   cups refrigerated prechopped
    celery, onion, and bell pepper mix
½   cup chopped carrot
2   garlic cloves, pressed
1½ lb. ground chuck
¾   tsp. salt
¾   tsp. freshly ground pepper
2   cups milk
1½ cups dry white wine
¼   tsp. freshly ground nutmeg
1   (28-oz.) can whole San Marzano
    tomatoes in tomato purée,
    undrained and chopped
Hot cooked pappardelle pasta
Freshly grated Parmesan cheese
    (optional)
Chopped fresh parsley (optional)

1. Heat oil in a large nonstick skillet over medium-high heat. Add celery mix and carrot; sauté 3 minutes or until tender. Add garlic; sauté 1 minute. Transfer vegetable mixture to a lightly greased 5-qt. slow cooker.

2. Add beef, salt, and pepper to skillet; cook 5 minutes, stirring until beef crumbles and is no longer pink. Add beef mixture to vegetable mixture. Stir in milk and next 3 ingredients.

3. Cover and cook on HIGH 6 hours. Serve sauce over hot cooked pasta; sprinkle with Parmesan cheese and parsley, if desired.

How to Chop Fresh Herbs

Don't worry about stemming cilantro, dill, or parsley; their stems are tender and can be chopped and used with the leaves. Simply place the bunch on a cutting board, and chop with a sharp knife.

Shortcut Ravioli Lasagna

Use your favorite pasta sauce for this ultra-easy dish. We liked the flavor of Newman's Own.

makes 4 to 6 servings • hands-on time: 15 min. • total time: 6 hr., 15 min.

1   lb. ground round
1   cup refrigerated prechopped onion
2   garlic cloves, minced (optional)
1   (24-oz.) jar pasta sauce
1   (25-oz.) package frozen cheese-filled ravioli (do not thaw)
1   (8-oz.) package shredded Italian six-cheese blend

1. Cook ground round, onion, and, if desired, garlic in a large skillet over medium-high heat until beef crumbles and is no longer pink. Drain, if needed.

2. Spoon ¾ cup pasta sauce into bottom of a lightly greased 4-qt. slow cooker. Layer half of ravioli, half of meat mixture, and 1 cup cheese over sauce. Repeat layers with ¾ cup sauce, remaining ravioli, and remaining meat mixture. Top with remaining sauce; sprinkle with remaining 1 cup cheese.

3. Cover and cook on LOW 6 hours or until pasta is tender.

Swedish Meatballs

makes 6 servings • hands-on time: 14 min. • total time: 3 hr., 14 min.

1 (32-oz.) package frozen fully cooked meatballs (do not thaw)
2 Tbsp. vegetable oil
¼ cup all-purpose flour
½ tsp. salt
¼ tsp. garlic powder
¼ tsp. freshly ground pepper
⅛ tsp. ground nutmeg
2 cups chicken broth
½ cup white wine
½ cup sour cream
2 Tbsp. chopped fresh parsley
½ cup red currant jelly (optional)
Hot cooked noodles
Garnish: chopped fresh parsley

1. Cook meatballs in a large skillet over medium-high heat, turning occasionally, 5 minutes or until browned on all sides.

2. Place meatballs in a 4-qt. slow cooker, reserving drippings in skillet. Reduce heat to low; add oil to skillet. Whisk in flour and next 4 ingredients until smooth. Increase heat to medium; cook, whisking constantly, 1 minute. Gradually whisk in chicken broth and wine. Cook, whisking frequently, 4 minutes or until slightly thickened. Pour gravy over meatballs. Cover and cook on LOW 3 hours.

3. Remove meatballs from slow cooker with a slotted spoon, and place in a serving bowl. Add sour cream, 2 Tbsp. parsley, and, if desired, jelly to gravy, whisking until blended. Pour over meatballs. Serve over hot cooked noodles; garnish, if desired.

Fruited Lamb Tagine

makes 4 servings • hands-on time: 15 min. • total time: 8 hr., 15 min.

2 Tbsp. all-purpose flour
2 tsp. garam masala
½ tsp. ground turmeric
½ tsp. salt
¼ tsp. pepper
2 lb. boneless leg of lamb, cut into ½-inch cubes
2 Tbsp. olive oil
1 (8-oz.) container refrigerated prechopped onion
1 (14-oz.) can beef broth
1 cup dried pitted plums
1 cup dried apricots
⅓ cup orange marmalade
Hot cooked couscous
Garnishes: chopped fresh cilantro, toasted slivered almonds

1. Combine first 5 ingredients in a large zip-top plastic freezer bag; add lamb. Seal bag, shaking to coat.

2. Heat oil in a large skillet over medium-high heat until hot; add lamb. Cook 2 minutes on each side or until browned.

3. Place lamb and onion in a 4- or 5-qt. slow cooker. Add broth and next 3 ingredients, stirring well. Cover and cook on LOW 8 hours or until meat is very tender. Serve over couscous. Garnish, if desired.

Secret Ingredient

Garam masala is a blend of Indian spices that are also found in North African, specifically Moroccan, dishes. Using a spice blend reduces the number of individual spices to purchase and measure for this recipe. Garam masala also makes a nice rub for chicken or salmon, or use it sparingly to flavor curries.

ideal slow cooker
5-quart

Braised Rosemary Lamb Chops

Greek seasoning combines oregano, mint, garlic, onion, black pepper, and lemon zest.

makes 4 servings • hands-on time: 13 min. • total time: 6 hr., 13 min.

4 lamb shoulder chops

4 tsp. Greek seasoning

2 Tbsp. olive oil

1 (8-oz.) container refrigerated prechopped celery, onion, and bell pepper mix

1 cup chicken broth

¼ cup chopped drained sun-dried tomatoes in oil

1 tsp. chopped fresh rosemary

¼ tsp. chili powder

1 (16-oz.) can chickpeas, drained

1 (14-oz.) can artichoke hearts, drained

Hot cooked couscous

Pine nuts, toasted

Garnish: lemon zest

1. Rub lamb chops on both sides with Greek seasoning. Heat oil in a medium skillet over medium-high heat. Add lamb; cook 3 minutes on each side or until browned.

2. Place lamb in a 5-qt. slow cooker, reserving drippings in skillet. Cook celery mix in hot drippings 2 minutes. Remove pan from heat. Add chicken broth and next 3 ingredients to pan, stirring to loosen particles from bottom of pan.

3. Add chickpeas and artichoke hearts to slow cooker. Pour broth mixture over lamb and vegetables. Cover and cook on LOW 6 hours or until lamb is tender. Serve over couscous. Sprinkle with pine nuts, and garnish, if desired.

ideal slow cooker
6-quart oval

Veal Chops with Figs

We tested this recipe using veal rib chops, but loin chops would work as well. The thicker the better here, since the meat simmers low and slow to melt-in-your-mouth tenderness.

makes 4 servings • hands-on time: 15 min. • total time: 6 hr., 15 min.

1 cup pomegranate juice
¾ cup sugar
6 garlic cloves, minced
1 Tbsp. chopped fresh thyme
1 tsp. coarsely ground or freshly ground pepper
4 (1- to 1½-inch-thick) veal rib chops
1 Tbsp. olive oil
2 shallots, vertically sliced
1 (8-oz.) package dried figs, coarsely chopped (1 cup)
1 Tbsp. balsamic vinegar
Garnish: fresh thyme

1. Combine pomegranate juice, sugar, and ¾ cup water in a saucepan. Bring to a boil over high heat. Boil 12 to 15 minutes or until syrupy. Set aside.

2. Meanwhile, combine garlic, thyme, and pepper; rub over veal. Heat oil in a large skillet over medium-high heat. Brown veal 2 minutes on each side.

3. Arrange veal in a lightly greased 6-qt. oval slow cooker, reserving drippings in skillet. Add shallots to skillet; toss gently. Cook 4 to 5 minutes or until soft. Spoon shallots and figs over veal. Pour reserved pomegranate syrup over figs. Drizzle with vinegar. Cover and cook on LOW 6 hours or until veal is tender. Garnish, if desired.

Sweet 'n' Spicy Braised Pork Tacos

makes 8 to 10 servings • hands-on time: 7 min. • total time: 10 hr., 17 min.

3   lb. boneless pork shoulder roast
     (Boston butt)
½   tsp. salt
½   tsp. freshly ground pepper
1   Tbsp. vegetable oil
2   (14½-oz.) cans diced tomatoes
     with garlic and onion
1   medium-size sweet onion, chopped
1   to 2 canned chipotle peppers in
     adobo sauce, chopped
2   Tbsp. cider vinegar
2   Tbsp. dark brown sugar
¼   tsp. ground cumin
Salt and pepper to taste
6   cups cooked white rice
1   (15-oz.) can black beans
16   to 20 (6-inch) fajita-size flour
     tortillas, warmed
Garnishes: fresh cilantro sprigs,
     lime wedges

1. Sprinkle pork with salt and pepper. Cook pork in hot oil in a large skillet over medium-high heat 2 to 3 minutes on all sides or until pork is browned. Stir together tomatoes and next 5 ingredients in a 5-qt. slow cooker. Add pork, turning to coat.

2. Cover and cook on LOW 10 hours or until pork is fork-tender. Transfer pork to a cutting board, and let stand 10 minutes. Shred pork with 2 forks. Return shredded pork to slow cooker, and stir until blended. Season with salt and pepper to taste. Serve immediately with a slotted spoon over rice and black beans in tortillas. Garnish, if desired.

**ideal slow cooker
5- or 6-quart oval**

Smoked Paprika Pork

Spanish smoked paprika is a popular spice in cooking stores. Known for its deep, smoky flavor without the heat, it's a marvelous accent for shrimp, roasted meats, and stews.

makes 6 servings • hands-on time: 12 min. • total time: 4 hr., 42 min.

3   large garlic cloves, pressed
1   tsp. Spanish smoked paprika
½   tsp. salt
½   tsp. ground cumin
¼   tsp. freshly ground pepper
1   Tbsp. olive oil
1   (2-lb.) package pork tenderloins
½   cup whipping cream
2   (8.8-oz.) pouches ready-to-serve
     long-grain and wild rice mix
2   bacon slices, cooked and coarsely
     crumbled
Chopped fresh chives

1. Combine first 5 ingredients. Stir in oil. Pat tenderloins dry with paper towels. Rub paprika mixture over tenderloins. Arrange in a greased 5- or 6-qt. oval slow cooker. Cover and cook on HIGH 1 hour. Reduce heat to LOW, and cook 3½ hours or until very tender.

2. Remove pork from slow cooker; cover and keep warm on a serving platter. Pour meat drippings into a large skillet. Bring to a boil over medium-high heat. Add whipping cream; boil until slightly thickened, 6 to 7 minutes.

3. Meanwhile, microwave rice according to package directions. Spoon rice around pork on platter. Remove sauce from heat; drizzle over pork. Sprinkle with bacon and chives.

ideal slow cooker
5-quart

Mediterranean Stuffed Pork Tenderloin

makes 6 servings • hands-on time: 15 min. • total time: 3 hr., 25 min.

⅓ cup drained sun-dried tomatoes in oil, chopped

3½ Tbsp. oil from sun-dried tomatoes, divided

1¼ tsp. salt, divided

¾ tsp. pepper, divided

1 Tbsp. dried Italian seasoning

2 Tbsp. chopped pitted kalamata olives

¾ tsp. lemon zest

2 garlic cloves, pressed

2 (1-lb.) pork tenderloins

½ cup crumbled feta cheese

1 (14½-oz.) can diced tomatoes with basil, garlic, and oregano, undrained

1 Tbsp. cornstarch

1. Place sun-dried tomatoes in a small bowl. Stir in 2 Tbsp. sun-dried tomato oil, 1 tsp. salt, ½ tsp. pepper, and next 4 ingredients. But-terfly pork by making a lengthwise cut down center of 1 side of each tenderloin, cutting to within ½ inch of other side. Unfold, forming 2 rectangles. Sprinkle each tenderloin with ⅛ tsp. salt and ⅛ tsp.pepper. Spread half of sun-dried tomato mixture over each tenderloin, leaving a ½-inch border; sprinkle with cheese. Fold long sides of tenderloins together to enclose filling; secure with wooden picks. Heat remaining 1½ Tbsp. sun-dried tomato oil in a skillet; add stuffed tenderloins. Cook, turning occasionally, 4 minutes or just until browned on all sides. Place tenderloins, seam side up, in a 5-qt. slow cooker; add diced tomatoes. Cover and cook on LOW 3 hours.

2. Remove tenderloins to a platter, reserving tomato mixture in slow cooker; cover and let stand 10 to 15 minutes before slicing.

3. Meanwhile, stir together cornstarch and 2 Tbsp. water until smooth; stir into tomato mixture. Increase heat to HIGH; cook 10 minutes or until slightly thickened. Remove wooden picks; cut tenderloins into slices. Spoon tomato gravy over pork slices.

Mushroom-and-Sausage Wild Rice with Pecans and Raisins

makes 6 servings • hands-on time: 15 min. • total time: 2 hr., 45 min.

1	lb. ground pork sausage
1	(8-oz.) container refrigerated prechopped onion
1	(8-oz.) package sliced fresh mushrooms
⅓	cup wild rice
3	cups chicken broth
2	cups converted long-grain rice
⅔	cup raisins
1½	tsp. chopped fresh thyme
½	tsp. kosher salt
½	tsp. freshly ground pepper
½	cup coarsely chopped pecans, toasted

1. Brown sausage in a large skillet over medium-high heat, stirring often, 5 minutes or until meat crumbles and is no longer pink; drain, reserving 2 tablespoons drippings in pan. Sauté onion, mushrooms, and wild rice in hot drippings 5 minutes or until vegetables are tender. Add broth to vegetables, stirring to loosen particles from bottom of skillet.

2. Place sausage, converted rice, and next 4 ingredients in a lightly greased 5-qt. slow cooker; stir in broth mixture. Cover and cook on LOW 2½ hours or until liquid is absorbed and rice is tender. Add pecans to rice; fluff with a fork.

Baked Four-Cheese Spaghetti with Italian Sausage

makes 8 to 10 servings • hands-on time: 15 min. • total time: 3 hr., 25 min. • pictured on page 190

8   oz. uncooked spaghetti

1   lb. Italian sausage (about 4 links)

1   (8-oz.) container refrigerated prechopped bell pepper and onion mix

2   tsp. jarred minced garlic

1   Tbsp. vegetable oil

1   (24-oz.) jar fire-roasted tomato and garlic pasta sauce

1   (16-oz.) package shredded sharp Cheddar cheese

1   (8-oz.) package shredded mozzarella cheese, divided

4   oz. fontina cheese, shredded

½   cup (2 oz.) preshredded Parmesan cheese

Garnish: fresh chopped basil

1. Cook pasta in boiling salted water in a large Dutch oven according to package directions. Drain and return to pan.

2. Meanwhile, brown sausage, bell pepper mix, and garlic in oil in a large nonstick skillet over medium-high heat, stirring often, 8 to 10 minutes or until meat crumbles and is no longer pink. Drain. Stir meat mixture, pasta sauce, and Cheddar cheese into pasta. Spoon half of pasta mixture into a lightly greased 5-qt. slow cooker.

3. Combine mozzarella cheese and fontina cheese. Sprinkle half of mozzarella mixture over pasta mixture in slow cooker. Top with remaining pasta mixture, remaining mozzarella mixture, and Parmesan cheese. Cover and cook on LOW 3 hours. Let stand, covered, 10 minutes before serving. Garnish, if desired.

How to Cook Perfect Pasta

If you can boil water, you can make great pasta. Most packages give directions, but here are some additional tips. Use a Dutch oven or stockpot  to allow room for the pasta to move freely in the boiling water and cook evenly. Use as much water as possible. For 8 ounces of dried pasta, use 4 quarts water.

Italian Sausage and Peppers with Rotini

makes 6 servings • hands-on time: 15 min. • total time: 8 hr., 15 min.

1 (19.5 oz.) package turkey Italian sausage links

1 cup finely chopped sweet onion

4 cloves garlic, finely chopped

2 medium yellow bell peppers, cut into ½-inch pieces

2 medium red bell peppers, cut into ½-inch pieces

1 (26-oz.) jar tomato pasta sauce

4½ cups (12 oz.) uncooked rotini pasta

6 Tbsp. shredded Parmesan cheese

1. Mix all ingredients except pasta and cheese in a lightly greased 3- or 4-qt. slow cooker. Cover and cook on LOW 6 to 8 hours.

2. Cook and drain pasta according to package directions. Serve sausage mixture over pasta; sprinkle each serving with 1 Tbsp. cheese.

Muffuletta Brunch Strata

makes 8 servings • hands-on time: 14 min. • total time: 3 hr., 39 min.

1 (32-oz.) jar garden mix olive salad, drained

1 (7-oz.) jar pimiento-stuffed Spanish olives, drained

1 slow-cooker liner

1 (1-lb.) peasant bread loaf, torn into bite-size pieces

1½ cups (6 oz.) shredded mozzarella cheese

1½ cups (6 oz.) shredded provolone cheese

1 (4-oz.) package sliced mortadella sausage, chopped (about 1¼ cups)

1 (4-oz.) package sliced Genoa salami, chopped (about 1¼ cups)

6 large eggs

3 cups milk

1 tsp. dried Italian seasoning

1. Pulse olive salad in a food processor until coarsely chopped. Transfer to a bowl. Process olives until coarsely chopped; add to bowl, tossing to combine.

2. Place liner in a 5-qt. slow cooker according to manufacturer's instructions. Layer one-third of bread in bottom of liner. Toss cheeses together in a bowl. Sprinkle bread with 1½ cups cheese mixture. Sprinkle cheese with half of olive salad mixture, half of mortadella, and half of salami. Repeat layers using one-third of bread and remaining cheese mixture, olive salad mixture, mortadella, and salami. Top with remaining one-third of bread.

3. Whisk eggs in a large bowl; whisk in milk and Italian seasoning. Pour egg mixture over bread in slow cooker until all bread is moistened. (Cooker will be full.) Cover and cook on HIGH 3 hours or until strata is puffed and set in center. Uncover and cook 15 more minutes. Remove liner and strata from cooker; let strata stand 10 minutes before serving.

Chicken Tostadas

You can serve all kinds of toppings, such as sour cream, salsa, chopped avocado, or cilantro, with this delicious dish.

makes 6 servings • hands-on time: 12 min. • total time: 7 hr., 12 min.

¾ cup chicken broth

½ cup salsa

⅓ cup all-purpose flour

1 large onion, chopped

2½ lb. skinned and boned chicken breasts

⅔ cup sour cream

Vegetable oil

6 (8-inch) flour tortillas

1 (8-oz.) bag shredded lettuce

1 (15-oz.) can red beans, heated

2 cups (8 oz.) shredded sharp Cheddar cheese

1 large tomato, chopped

1. Combine broth, salsa, and flour in a 5-qt. slow cooker, whisking to blend. Stir in onion. Arrange chicken in slow cooker, smooth side up. Cover and cook on HIGH 1 hour; reduce heat to LOW, and cook 6 hours. Remove chicken from cooker and shred; stir in sour cream.

2. Return chicken mixture to slow cooker. Keep warm.

3. Pour oil to a depth of ¼ inch in a heavy skillet. Fry tortillas, 1 at a time, in hot oil over high heat 20 seconds on each side or until crisp and golden brown. Drain on paper towels.

4. Layer lettuce, beans, chicken mixture, cheese, and chopped tomato on warm tortillas.

Sesame Chicken

makes 4 to 6 servings • hands-on time: 7 min. • total time: 2 hr., 37 min.

1¼ cups chicken broth

½ cup firmly packed brown sugar

¼ cup cornstarch

2 Tbsp. rice vinegar

2 Tbsp. soy sauce

2 Tbsp. sweet chili sauce

2 Tbsp. honey

2 tsp. dark sesame oil

1½ lb. skinned and boned chicken breasts, cut into 1-inch pieces

2 cups sugar snap peas

2 cups crinkle-cut carrots

1½ Tbsp. sesame seeds, toasted

Hot cooked rice

Garnish: chopped green onions

1. Whisk together first 8 ingredients in a 4-qt. slow cooker. Stir in chicken. Cover and cook on HIGH 2½ hours or until chicken is done, stirring after 1½ hours.

2. Steam sugar snap peas and carrots. Stir vegetable mixture and sesame seeds into slow cooker. Serve over hot cooked rice. Garnish, if desired.

ideal slow cooker
5-quart

Creamy Mustard Chicken with Leeks

Cream of chicken soup is the base for this recipe's sauce. Cream of celery or cream of mushroom soup would taste fine as well.

makes 6 servings • hands-on time: 13 min. • total time: 3 hr., 13 min.

2   medium leeks, sliced
2   Tbsp. olive oil
6   skinned and boned chicken breasts
¾   tsp. salt, divided
¾   tsp. freshly ground pepper, divided
¼   cup whipping cream
3   Tbsp. coarse-grained mustard
5   garlic cloves, minced
1   (10¾-oz.) can cream of chicken soup
Hot cooked rice

1. Place leeks in a lightly greased 5-qt. slow cooker.

2. Heat oil in a large nonstick skillet over medium-high heat. Sprinkle chicken with ½ tsp. each salt and pepper. Sauté chicken, in 2 batches, 2 minutes on each side or until browned. Place chicken in slow cooker.

3. Combine remaining ¼ tsp. each of salt and pepper, whipping cream, and next 3 ingredients; pour over chicken in slow cooker. Cover and cook on LOW 3 hours. Serve over hot cooked rice.

Chicken with Wine-Mushroom Gravy

Searing chicken breasts briefly in a hot skillet gives you a jump-start on cooking and developing rich flavor.

makes 6 servings • hands-on time: 15 min. • total time: 3 hr., 15 min.

6 skinned and boned chicken breasts
¼ tsp. salt
¼ tsp. pepper
1 Tbsp. olive oil
1 (8-oz.) package sliced fresh mushrooms
1 large shallot, minced
1 cup dry white wine
1 (10¾-oz.) can cream of mushroom soup
2 cups sour cream
2 Tbsp. chopped fresh parsley

1. Sprinkle chicken with salt and pepper. Heat oil in a large skillet over medium-high heat. Add chicken to skillet; cook 3 minutes on each side or until browned. Place chicken in a lightly greased 5-qt. slow cooker.

2. Add mushrooms to skillet; sauté over high heat 4 minutes or until browned. Add shallot; cook 1 minute. Whisk in wine and soup until blended. Pour mushroom mixture over chicken.

3. Cover and cook on LOW 3 hours or until chicken is done. Transfer chicken to a serving platter. Stir sour cream into juices in slow cooker; spoon over chicken. Sprinkle with parsley.

Hungarian Chicken with Smoked Paprika

makes 4 servings • hands-on time: 22 min. • total time: 6 hr., 22 min.

1   red bell pepper, cored, seeded, and sliced

1   yellow bell pepper, cored, seeded, and sliced

1   onion, sliced

1   (28-oz.) can diced tomatoes, drained, with ½ cup juice reserved

1   cup chicken broth, divided

1   garlic clove, minced

1   tsp. picante Spanish smoked paprika or 1½ tsp. Hungarian paprika

1   Tbsp. plus 2 tsp. olive oil

1   (3-lb.) chicken, quartered and skinned

1   Tbsp. kosher salt

½   tsp. pepper

⅓   cup sour cream

Hot cooked pasta

1. Place peppers, onion, tomatoes and reserved juice, ½ cup broth, garlic, and paprika in a 6-qt. slow cooker. Heat oil in a large skillet over medium-high heat. Sprinkle chicken with salt and pepper. Add to skillet, and cook 8 minutes or until browned. Transfer to slow cooker. Pour remaining ½ cup broth into skillet; cook 2 minutes, stirring to loosen particles from bottom of skillet. Pour liquid into slow cooker; cover and cook on HIGH 6 hours.

2. Remove chicken, and let cool. Remove meat from bones, and return meat to slow cooker; discard bones. Stir in sour cream. Serve chicken over hot cooked pasta.

Slow-Cooker School

Be sure not to add the sour cream until the dish has finished cooking. Dairy products can curdle if exposed to high heat for very long.

Lemon-Rosemary Chicken

Rather than removing the slow-cooker lid to check on the chicken, it's best to gently tap the lid to release the condensation so you can see inside.

makes 4 servings • hands-on time: 7 min. • total time: 4 hr., 49 min.

1   (4-lb.) chicken
1   lemon, halved
3   sprigs fresh rosemary
2   garlic cloves
3   Tbsp. unsalted butter, divided
Salt and pepper
Garnishes: lemon wedges, fresh
    rosemary

1. Rinse chicken, and pat dry. Place lemon, rosemary, garlic, and 2 Tbsp. butter inside cavity of chicken. Fold wingtips under chicken, and tie legs together with string. Sprinkle chicken with salt and pepper.

2. Place chicken, breast side up, on a small rack inside a 5-qt. oval slow cooker. Cook on HIGH 4 to 4½ hours or until an instant-read thermometer inserted into thigh registers 170°.

3. Preheat broiler. Melt remaining 1 Tbsp. butter. Transfer chicken, breast side up, to an aluminum foil-lined baking sheet. Brush chicken with melted butter, and broil to brown skin 2 to 3 minutes. Let stand 10 minutes on a cutting board before carving and serving. Garnish, if desired.

ideal slow cooker
6-quart

Creamy Thyme Chicken and Winter Vegetables

Slow cooking root vegetables beneath juicy chicken thighs allows the meat juices to drip down and impart great flavor.

makes 4 servings • hands-on time: 15 min. • total time: 5 hr., 15 min.

8 skinned chicken thighs

1 (8-oz.) package frozen prechopped onion

1 lb. Yukon gold potatoes, peeled and sliced

1 lb. sweet potatoes, peeled and sliced

1 lb. rutabagas, peeled and sliced

2 (10¾-oz.) cans cream of chicken soup

1 tsp. salt

½ tsp. dried thyme

½ tsp. pepper

4 oz. goat cheese

½ cup Italian-seasoned breadcrumbs

Garnish: fresh thyme

1. Preheat broiler with oven rack 5½ inches from heat. Place chicken on a lightly greased rack in an aluminum foil-lined broiler pan. Broil 10 minutes.

2. Meanwhile, layer onion, potatoes, and rutabaga in a 6-qt. slow cooker. Stir together soup and next 3 ingredients in a medium bowl; pour over vegetables. Top with chicken.

3. Combine goat cheese and breadcrumbs. Sprinkle over chicken. Cover and cook on LOW 5 hours or until vegetables are tender. Garnish, if desired.

Plum-Glazed Chicken with Caramelized Shallots

Substitute brandy or apple juice for the Calvados or apple brandy, if desired.

makes 4 servings • hands-on time: 15 min. • total time: 6 hr., 20 min.

8   chicken thighs (about 3 lb.)

½   tsp. salt, divided

½   tsp. freshly ground pepper, divided

2   Tbsp. butter

8   large shallots, peeled

¼   cup Calvados or apple brandy

1   cup dried pitted plums

½   cup chicken broth

2   tsp. chopped fresh thyme

Hot cooked long-grain and wild rice

Garnish: fresh thyme sprigs

1. Preheat broiler with oven rack 5½ inches from heat. Sprinkle chicken with ¼ tsp. salt and ¼ tsp. pepper. Place chicken, skin side up, on a lightly greased rack in lightly greased broiler pan. Broil 10 minutes or until browned. Transfer chicken to a 5-qt. slow cooker.

2. Meanwhile, melt butter in a large skillet over medium-high heat. Add shallots; cook 8 minutes or until caramelized, turning occasionally. Add brandy, and cook 2 minutes or until liquid is reduced by half, stirring to loosen particles from bottom of skillet.

3. Add shallot mixture, remaining ¼ tsp. salt, remaining ¼ tsp. pepper, plums, chicken broth, and chopped thyme to slow cooker. Cover and cook on LOW 6 hours or until chicken is tender. Serve over hot cooked long-grain and wild rice. Garnish, if desired.

Orange Chicken with Potatoes

makes 4 to 6 servings • hands-on time: 12 min. • total time: 2 hr., 42 min.

8	skinned chicken thighs
1	tsp. kosher salt
½	tsp. pepper
1	onion, cut into eighths
1	lb. small red potatoes, halved
1	small butternut squash, peeled, seeded, and cut into 1-inch pieces
1	tsp. jarred minced garlic
1	orange, cut into ¼-inch slices
1	cup low-sodium chicken broth
1	Tbsp. honey
8	sprigs thyme

1. Rinse chicken and pat dry with paper towels; season with salt and pepper. Brown chicken in a large skillet over medium-high heat 4 minutes on each side.

2. Combine chicken, onion, potato, and remaining ingredients in a 6-qt. slow cooker. Cover and cook on HIGH 2½ hours or on LOW 5 hours.

Braised Chicken Thighs with Carrots and Potatoes

Substitute an extra ¼ cup chicken broth for the wine, if you prefer.

makes 6 servings • hands-on time: 11 min. • total time: 7 hr., 11 min.

1	medium onion, halved lengthwise and sliced
4	medium-size new potatoes (about 1 lb.), cut into ¼-inch-thick slices
1	lb. baby carrots
1¼	tsp. salt, divided
½	tsp. pepper, divided
¼	cup chicken broth
¼	cup dry white wine
1	tsp. jarred minced garlic
½	tsp. dried thyme
1	tsp. paprika
1½	lb. skinned chicken thighs

Garnish: fresh thyme

1. Place onion in a lightly greased 6-qt. slow cooker; top with potatoes and carrots. Combine ¾ tsp. salt, ¼ tsp. pepper, broth, and next 3 ingredients. Pour broth mixture over vegetables. Combine paprika, remaining ½ tsp. salt, and remaining ¼ tsp. pepper; rub over chicken thighs, and arrange on top of vegetables.

2. Cover and cook on HIGH 1 hour; reduce heat to LOW, and cook 6 hours or until chicken and vegetables are tender. Garnish, if desired.

Mediterranean Chicken with Olives and Tomatoes

makes 4 servings • hands-on time: 13 min. • total time: 3 hr., 13 min.

4   chicken leg quarters (about 4 lb.)

1   tsp. kosher salt

½   tsp. freshly ground pepper

1   small lemon

½   cup pimiento-stuffed Spanish olives, halved

½   cup pitted kalamata olives, halved

1   Tbsp. chopped fresh thyme

2   Tbsp. jarred minced garlic

1   (14½-oz.) can diced tomatoes with basil, garlic, and oregano, undrained

3   oz. feta cheese, crumbled (optional)

1. Rinse chicken, and pat dry. Sprinkle chicken with salt and pepper. Heat a large nonstick skillet over medium-high heat. Add chicken to pan; cook 3 minutes on each side or until browned. Transfer chicken to a 5-qt. slow cooker, discarding drippings.

2. Grate zest and squeeze juice from lemon to measure 1 tsp. zest and 1 Tbsp. juice. Stir together lemon zest, lemon juice, olives, and next 3 ingredients in a medium bowl. Pour over chicken. Cover and cook on LOW 3 hours or until chicken is tender. Sprinkle chicken with cheese, if desired.

How to Zest a Lemon

To zest a lemon, rub the lemon in one direction against the blade of a fine grater. Be sure to zest just the yellow part of the lemon and not the bitter white pith beneath.

ideal slow cooker
4-quart

Spicy Asian Barbecued Drummettes

Look for sriracha hot chili sauce with the Asian foods on grocery shelves. It's a staple on the kitchen table in parts of Asia—much like ketchup is in the U.S. The blend of chiles, garlic, sugar, salt, and vinegar is very spicy.

makes 2 to 4 servings • hands-on time: 8 min. • total time: 3 hr., 8 min. • pictured on cover

3 lb. chicken drummettes (about 20)
½ tsp. salt
¼ tsp. pepper
1 cup honey-barbecue sauce
1 Tbsp. sriracha hot chili sauce
1 Tbsp. soy sauce
3 garlic cloves, pressed
Garnishes: toasted sesame seeds,
    sliced green onions (optional)

1. Preheat broiler with oven rack 3 inches from heat.

2. Sprinkle drummettes with salt and pepper. Place on a lightly greased rack in a broiler pan. Broil 8 minutes or until browned. Place drummettes in a 4-qt. slow cooker.

3. Combine barbecue sauce and next 3 ingredients; pour over drummettes. Cover and cook on LOW 3 hours. Garnish, if desired. Serve with sauce for dipping.

How to Toast Sesame Seeds

Toast sesame seeds in a medium-size pan over medium-high heat. Toast seeds, stirring frequently, for 2 to 3 minutes or until brown and fragrant.

Apple Butter-Glazed Turkey

Boneless turkey tenderloins cook faster and don't need carving like a bone-in turkey breast.

makes 4 servings • hands-on time: 10 min. • total time: 6 hr., 10 min.

2 lb. large carrots, cut into ½-inch slices

4 (1-lb.) turkey tenderloins

1 cup firmly packed dark brown sugar

½ cup apple butter

¼ cup frozen orange juice concentrate, thawed

2 tsp. pumpkin pie spice

1 tsp. kosher salt

2 Tbsp. cornstarch

Garnish: orange zest

1. Place carrots in a 5-qt. slow cooker. Arrange turkey over carrots.

2. Combine brown sugar and next 4 ingredients. Pour mixture over turkey tenderloins. Cover and cook on HIGH 1 hour.

3. Reduce heat to LOW, and cook 5 hours or until turkey and carrots are tender.

4. Place turkey and carrots on a serving platter. Pour juices through a wire-mesh strainer into a 3-qt. saucepan. Bring to a boil. Whisk together cornstarch and 3 Tbsp. water until smooth. Gradually whisk cornstarch mixture into juices. Cook 1 minute or until thickened, whisking constantly. Serve sauce over turkey and carrots. Garnish, if desired.

Turkey and Dressing

makes 6 servings   •   hands-on time: 15 min.   •   total time: 6 hr., 15 min.

1 (3-lb.) frozen skin-on, boned turkey breast

1 (8-oz.) package herb-seasoned stuffing mix

1½ cups refrigerated prechopped celery, onion, and bell pepper mix

½ cup dried apricots, coarsely chopped

½ cup dried dates, chopped

2 Tbsp. chopped fresh rosemary

¾ cup coarsely chopped pecans

¾ cup chicken broth

3 Tbsp. butter, melted

2 Tbsp. butter, softened

¼ tsp. salt

¼ tsp. pepper

1 (0.88-oz.) package turkey gravy mix

Garnish: fresh rosemary

1. Thaw turkey breast in refrigerator, and follow basic preparation directions.

2. Place stuffing mix and next 5 ingredients in a lightly greased 4-qt. slow cooker. Combine broth and melted butter. Pour over stuffing, stirring gently.

3. Rinse and pat turkey dry with paper towels. Place turkey, breast side up, over dressing. Rub softened butter over turkey breast; sprinkle with salt and pepper. Cover and cook on HIGH 1 hour. Reduce heat to LOW, and cook 5 hours or until a meat thermometer inserted into thigh registers 170°.

4. Place turkey on a platter; cover with aluminum foil. Stir stuffing; cover and let stand 4 minutes.

5. Meanwhile, prepare gravy mix according to package directions. Spoon stuffing around turkey on platter. Serve with gravy. Garnish, if desired.

Lemon Trout in Creamy White Wine Sauce

The trout fillets may overlap in the bottom of the slow cooker, but make sure that the edges do not come in direct contact with the sides of the cooker and that they are covered with sauce so they won't dry out.

makes 4 servings • hands-on time: 5 min. • total time: 2 hr., 35 min.

1½ lb. trout fillets
½   tsp. salt, divided
½   tsp. freshly ground pepper, divided
¼   cup butter
1   tsp. jarred minced garlic
2   Tbsp. all-purpose flour
⅔   cup milk
⅓   cup dry white wine
1   Tbsp. lemon zest
1   Tbsp. sugar
Hot cooked wild rice
Garnishes: lemon slices, chopped
    fresh parsley, capers

1. Sprinkle fish with ⅛ tsp. salt and ⅛ tsp. pepper, and arrange in bottom of a lightly greased 4-qt. slow cooker.

2. Melt butter in a small heavy saucepan over medium heat. Add garlic, and sauté 30 seconds. Whisk in flour until smooth. Cook 1 minute, whisking constantly. Gradually whisk in milk, wine, and zest; cook over medium heat, whisking constantly, until mixture is thickened and bubbly. Stir in remaining ⅜ tsp. salt, remaining ⅜ tsp. pepper, and sugar. Pour sauce over fish. Cover and cook on HIGH 2½ hours or just until fish flakes with a fork. Serve over hot cooked wild rice. Garnish, if desired.

Orange-Rosemary Poached Salmon

Select fillets from the ends of the salmon. These are thinner than those cut from the center of the fish.

makes 4 servings • hands-on time: 9 min • total time: 2 hr., 39 min.

1 cup orange juice
1 cup vegetable broth
½ cup fresh parsley leaves
3 Tbsp. butter
6 garlic cloves, pressed
2 (5-inch) sprigs fresh rosemary
1 navel orange, sliced
4 (6-oz.) skinless salmon fillets (½ to ¾ inch thick)
1 tsp. salt
2 tsp. orange zest
½ tsp. freshly ground black pepper
¼ tsp. ground red pepper
Hot cooked orzo
Sautéed baby bok choy

1. Place first 7 ingredients in a 5-qt. oval slow cooker. Cover and cook on HIGH 2 hours.

2. Meanwhile, sprinkle salmon with salt, orange zest, and peppers. Cover and chill 2 hours.

3. Place salmon in liquid in slow cooker. Cover and cook 30 more minutes or until desired degree of doneness. Carefully transfer salmon to a serving platter using a large spatula. Serve over hot cooked orzo and sautéed baby bok choy.

ideal slow cooker
6-quart oval

Greek Snapper

makes 4 servings • hands-on time: 9 min. • total time: 3 hr., 9 min.

1½ cups dry white wine
1 cup thinly sliced onion
3 garlic cloves, minced
2 bay leaves
4 (6-oz.) red snapper fillets (1 inch thick)
4 plum tomatoes, chopped
1 tsp. dried oregano
½ tsp. salt
½ tsp. freshly ground pepper
1 Tbsp. olive oil
Hot cooked rice
1 oz. crumbled feta cheese
Lemon wedges
Garnish: fresh oregano

1. Combine first 4 ingredients in a 6-qt. oval slow cooker. Cover and cook on HIGH 1 hour.

2. Add fish to slow cooker in a single layer. Combine tomato and next 3 ingredients in a bowl; spoon over fish. Drizzle olive oil over fish. Reduce heat to LOW; cover and cook 2 hours.

3. Carefully remove fish from cooking liquid. Serve over rice. Spoon tomato mixture over fish. Sprinkle with feta cheese, and serve with lemon wedges. Garnish, if desired.

Slow-Cooker School

Heating the poaching liquid on HIGH for 1 hour brings it to the perfect temperature to poach the fish in 2 hours. For best results, use an oval slow cooker; it will provide more surface area to arrange the fish in a single layer.

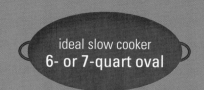

ideal slow cooker
6- or 7-quart oval

Crab Dip-Stuffed Mushrooms

Choose mushrooms that are 4 inches in diameter with deep cavities to adequately hold the generous stuffing. Lump crabmeat is more economical than jumbo lump crabmeat, but the larger pieces make it easier to pick out the shells.

makes 4 servings • hands-on time: 11 min. • total time: 2 hr., 11 min.

1   lb. fresh lump crabmeat, drained
1   (8-oz.) package cream cheese, softened
⅓   cup sour cream
¼   cup mayonnaise
2   Tbsp. chopped fresh parsley
2   Tbsp. fresh lemon juice
1   tsp. Old Bay seasoning
2   tsp. Worcestershire sauce
¼   tsp. salt
¼   tsp. freshly ground pepper
4   large portobello mushrooms, stemmed
1   cup (4 oz.) shredded Swiss cheese
Garnishes: chopped fresh parsley, lemon wedges

1. Pick crabmeat, removing any bits of shell. Place cream cheese and next 8 ingredients in a bowl. Beat at medium speed with an electric mixer until blended; gently fold in crabmeat.

2. Using a spoon, scrape and discard brown gills from undersides of mushrooms, leaving edges of caps intact. Spoon crabmeat mixture into mushroom caps. Arrange mushrooms in a single layer in a lightly greased 6- or 7-qt. oval slow cooker. Sprinkle with cheese. Cover and cook on LOW 2 hours or until mushrooms are tender. Garnish, if desired.

Black-eyed Pea Soup,
page 280

Make It
Meatless

Savory Italian Vegetable Bread Pudding

If you're a fan of sweet bread pudding for dessert, try this savory version. It has a similar texture, but it's cheesy and loaded with flavor.

makes 6 servings • hands-on time: 8 min. • total time: 3 hr., 23 min.

1 Tbsp. olive oil

1 large zucchini, cubed

1 red bell pepper, chopped

1 small onion, chopped

6 large eggs

1 cup half-and-half

1½ tsp. Dijon mustard

1 tsp. dried Italian seasoning

½ tsp. salt

¼ tsp. pepper

1 (9½-oz.) package frozen mozzarella and Monterey Jack cheese Texas toast, cut into 1-inch cubes

1 cup (4 oz.) shredded Italian six-cheese blend

1. Heat a large skillet over medium-high heat. Add oil. Sauté zucchini and next 2 ingredients 5 minutes or until crisp-tender.

2. Whisk together eggs and next 5 ingredients.

3. Layer half of Texas toast in a lightly greased 5-qt. slow cooker; top with half of zucchini mixture and ½ cup cheese. Repeat layers. Pour egg mixture over all ingredients. Cover and cook on LOW 3 hours and 15 minutes or until set.

Vegetable Moussaka

makes 8 to 10 servings • hands-on time: 15 min. • total time: 8 hr., 15 min.

¼　cup butter

¼　cup all-purpose flour

3　cups milk

1½　cups (6 oz.) shredded Parmesan cheese, divided

2　large eggs

2　egg yolks

½　tsp. salt

½　tsp. freshly ground pepper

1　(1½-lb.) eggplant, peeled and cubed

1½　cups refrigerated presliced onion

1　(8-oz.) package sliced baby portobello mushrooms

1　(20-oz.) package refrigerated sliced potatoes

4　cups chunky spaghetti sauce

Garnish: fresh chopped parsley

1. Melt butter in a heavy saucepan over low heat; whisk in flour until smooth. Cook 2 minutes, whisking constantly. Gradually whisk in milk; cook over medium heat 3 to 4 minutes, whisking constantly, until mixture is thickened and bubbly. Stir in ½ cup Parmesan cheese. Gradually whisk together eggs, egg yolks, salt, and pepper in a medium bowl. Gradually stir about one-fourth of hot cheese mixture into egg mixture; add egg mixture to remaining hot cheese mixture, whisking constantly.

2. Arrange eggplant in bottom of a 7-qt. slow cooker. Layer onion, mushrooms, and potatoes over eggplant; pour spaghetti sauce over vegetables. Top with cheese sauce and remaining 1 cup cheese. Cover and cook on LOW 8 hours or until vegetables are tender. Garnish, if desired.

Shepherd's Pie

makes 6 servings • hands-on time: 8 min. • total time: 4 hr., 8 min.

2 (12-oz.) packages frozen meatless burger crumbles

2 Tbsp. all-purpose flour

1 (14½-oz.) can diced tomatoes with basil, garlic, and oregano, undrained

1 (16-oz.) package frozen peas and carrots

1 tsp. dried minced onion

1 (24-oz.) package refrigerated sour cream and chive mashed potatoes

1 cup (4 oz.) shredded sharp Cheddar cheese

Garnish: fresh chives

1. Toss together burger crumbles and flour in a large bowl until crumbles are coated. Stir in tomatoes and next 2 ingredients. Spoon mixture into a lightly greased 4-qt. slow cooker.

2. Microwave potatoes 1 minute according to package directions; stir and spread over vegetable mixture in slow cooker. Cover and cook on LOW 4 hours. Increase heat to HIGH. Sprinkle cheese over potatoes; cover and cook 7 minutes or until cheese melts. Garnish, if desired.

Veggie Chili and Potato Tot Nachos

makes 8 to 10 servings • hands-on time: 6 min. • total time: 3 hr., 6 min.

1   (22-oz.) package frozen potato tots

1   cup refrigerated prechopped onion

2   (15-oz.) cans vegetarian chili with beans

1   (12-oz.) package frozen meatless burger crumbles

3   cups (12 oz.) shredded Cheddar cheese, divided

½   cup drained pickled jalapeño pepper slices (optional)

1. Place half of potato tots in a lightly greased 4- or 5-qt. slow cooker. Combine onion, chili, and crumbles; stir well. Spoon chili mixture over potato tots. Sprinkle with 1½ cups cheese. Top with remaining potato tots. Cover and cook on LOW 3 hours.

2. Uncover and sprinkle with remaining 1½ cups cheese and, if desired, jalapeño slices.

Slow-Cooker School

Potato tots replace chips as the base for these cheesy nachos. Keep the finished dish on the warm setting up to 2 hours—the potato tots will begin to fall apart after lengthy heating.

Mediterranean Soufflé Casserole

You'll use partial cans of olives and artichoke hearts for this recipe. Plan on home-made pizza a few nights later to make good use of these leftover veggies.

makes 6 servings • hands-on time: 7 min. • total time: 3 hr., 17 min.

1 (12-oz.) jar roasted red bell peppers, drained and chopped

1 cup quartered artichoke hearts, chopped

½ cup sliced black olives

1 cup crumbled feta cheese

¼ cup evaporated milk

2 Tbsp. plain Greek yogurt

9 large eggs, lightly beaten

Freshly ground pepper

2 Tbsp. chopped fresh basil

1. Layer red bell peppers, artichoke hearts, and olives in a lightly greased 3- or 4-qt. slow cooker. Combine cheese and next 3 ingredients; stir well, and pour over vegetables in slow cooker. Sprinkle with pepper. Cover and cook on LOW 3 hours or just until egg is set in center.

2. Turn off cooker. Let stand, covered, 10 minutes. Sprinkle with basil before serving.

Sweet Potato Breakfast Bake

Quickly thaw sweet potatoes by snipping off a corner of the bag and microwaving at HIGH 3 minutes.

makes 8 servings • hands-on time: 9 min. • total time: 4 hr., 9 min.

2   Tbsp. butter, divided

1   (14-oz.) package soy sausage

6   large eggs

2   cups half-and-half

1   tsp. dried Italian seasoning

2   cups herb-seasoned stuffing mix

2   cups (8 oz.) shredded mozzarella
     cheese, divided

1   cup refrigerated prechopped onion

1   (24-oz.) package steam-and-mash
     frozen cut sweet potatoes, thawed

Garnish: chopped fresh parsley

1. Melt 1 Tbsp. butter in a large skillet over medium-high heat. Brown sausage in melted butter, stirring often, 5 to 6 minutes or until sausage crumbles and is browned.

2. Meanwhile, whisk together eggs and next 2 ingredients in a medium bowl.

3. Grease a 5-qt. slow cooker with remaining 1 Tbsp. butter. Stir together sausage, egg mixture, stuffing mix, 1 cup cheese, and next 2 ingredients in slow cooker. Top with remaining 1 cup cheese. Cover and cook on LOW 4 hours or until set and edges are browned. Garnish, if desired.

Wild Mushroom Pasta Alfredo with Walnuts

Agnolotti are square ravioli packets typically filled with meat, vegetables, or a combination of both.

makes 8 servings • hands-on time: 6 min. • total time: 2 hr., 6 min.

2 (15-oz.) jars Alfredo sauce
2 (9-oz.) packages refrigerated wild mushroom agnolotti pasta
1 cup (4 oz.) shredded Parmesan cheese
4 cups grape tomatoes
1 cup walnut halves, toasted
Freshly ground pepper
4 cups baby spinach
Garnish: shredded Parmesan cheese

1. Spoon 1 cup Alfredo sauce into a lightly greased 3½- or 4-qt. slow cooker. Spread 1 package of pasta over sauce. Top with ½ cup cheese, 2 cups tomatoes, and ½ cup walnuts. Sprinkle with pepper. Repeat layers once. Top with 1 cup Alfredo sauce. Reserve remaining Alfredo sauce for another use.

2. Cover and cook on HIGH 2 hours. Stir in spinach just before serving. Garnish, if desired.

ideal slow cooker
5-quart

Eggplant and Tomato Sauce with Pasta

When selecting eggplant, look for one that is shiny and smooth with no bruises. Store it, unwrapped, in the crisper section of your refrigerator.

makes 6 servings • hands-on time: 10 min. • total time: 4 hr., 22 min.

1   (28-oz.) can diced tomatoes, drained
1   (6-oz.) can tomato paste
½   cup red wine or water
1   medium eggplant (about 1 lb.), cut into ½-inch cubes
1   onion, finely chopped
2   garlic cloves, finely chopped
1   tsp. dried oregano
½   tsp. salt
1   (16-oz.) package rotini pasta
Garnish: grated Parmesan cheese

1. Combine tomatoes and next 7 ingredients in a 5-qt. slow cooker; cover and cook on LOW 4 hours or until eggplant is soft and sauce is thick.

2. Just before sauce is done, bring a large pot of salted water to a boil over high heat. Add pasta, and cook until al dente, about 10 minutes. Drain pasta, and toss with sauce. Garnish, if desired.

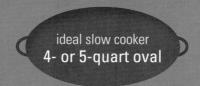

Pastitsio

Pastitsio is flavored with a long list of spices, but we've shortened the list with the combination of spices found in apple pie spice.

makes 4 to 6 servings • hands-on time: 15 min. • total time: 3 hr., 15 min.

2½   cups uncooked ziti pasta

1¼   cups chopped onion

3   garlic cloves, minced

2   tsp. olive oil

1   (12-oz.) package frozen meatless burger crumbles, thawed

1½   cups puttanesca-flavored pasta sauce

½   tsp. apple pie spice

½   tsp. salt

¼   tsp. freshly ground pepper

1   (8-oz.) package feta cheese, coarsely crumbled

1   (15-oz.) jar Alfredo sauce

3   large eggs

⅓   cup (1½ oz.) shredded Parmesan cheese

Garnishes: sliced black olives, fresh oregano leaves

1. Cook pasta according to package directions and drain.

2. Sauté onion and garlic in hot oil in a large skillet over medium heat 5 minutes or until tender. Remove pan from heat; stir in meatless crumbles and next 4 ingredients. Add pasta, stirring well. Gently stir in feta cheese.

3. Spoon mixture into a greased 4- or 5-qt. oval slow cooker. Whisk together Alfredo sauce and eggs in a bowl; pour over pasta mixture. Sprinkle Parmesan cheese over sauce. Cover and cook on LOW 3 hours or until lightly browned and bubbly. Garnish, if desired.

Thyme-Scented White Bean Cassoulet

makes 6 servings • hands-on time: 15 min. • total time: 8 hr., 15 min.

1   Tbsp. olive oil

1½   cups chopped onion

1½   cups (½-inch-thick) carrot slices,
     diagonally cut

1   cup (½-inch-thick) parsnip slices,
     diagonally cut

2   garlic cloves, minced

3   cups cooked great Northern
     beans

¾   cup vegetable broth

½   tsp. dried thyme

¼   tsp. salt

¼   tsp. pepper

1   (28-oz.) can diced tomatoes,
     undrained

1   bay leaf

¼   cup fine dry breadcrumbs

¼   cup (1 oz.) shredded Parmesan
     cheese

2   Tbsp. butter, melted

2   links meatless Italian sausage,
     thawed and chopped

2   Tbsp. chopped fresh parsley

1. Heat oil in a large nonstick skillet over medium heat. Add onion, carrot, parsnip, and garlic; cover and cook 5 minutes or until tender.

2. Place in a 5-qt. slow cooker. Add beans and next 6 ingredients. Cover and cook on LOW 8 hours or until vegetables are tender. Discard bay leaf.

3. Combine breadcrumbs, cheese, and butter in a small bowl; toss with a fork until moistened. Stir breadcrumb mixture and sausage into bean mixture; sprinkle with parsley.

ideal slow cooker
4-quart

Chickpea and Vegetable Tagine

makes 8 servings • hands-on time: 3 min. • total time: 10 hr., 3 min.

2 cups baby carrots
1 (8-oz.) container refrigerated prechopped onion
1 (14½-oz.) can diced tomatoes with garlic
2 (15½-oz.) cans chickpeas
½ cup sliced pitted Spanish olives
2 cups organic vegetable broth
1 tsp. ground cumin
¼ tsp. ground ginger
¼ tsp. ground turmeric
1 (3-inch) cinnamon stick
½ cup golden raisins (optional)
½ cup whole roasted, salted almonds (optional)
Garnish: chopped fresh parsley

1. Sir together first 10 ingredients in a 4-qt. slow cooker. Cover and cook on LOW 8 to 10 hours or until vegetables are tender. Remove and discard cinnamon stick. If desired, stir in raisins, and sprinkle with almonds. Garnish, if desired.

Slow-Cooker School

A tagine is a Moroccan entrée cooked low and slow in a cone-shaped ceramic dish by the same name. A slow cooker perfectly duplicates the flavorful results.

Cheesy Grits with Butternut Squash

makes 8 to 10 servings • hands-on time: 4 min. • total time: 4 hr., 4 min.

2 cups uncooked regular yellow grits
1 cup whipping cream
1 tsp. salt
1 (32-oz.) container vegetable broth
1 (15-oz.) can butternut squash puree
1 (10¾-oz.) can Cheddar cheese soup
¼ cup butter, cut into 4 pieces
Finely shredded sharp Cheddar cheese

1. Stir together first 6 ingredients in a lightly greased 4-qt. slow cooker until blended. Cover and cook on LOW 4 hours, stirring after 2 hours. Stir in butter, and sprinkle with cheese.

Slow-Cooker School

Slow cookers are known for producing creamy grits. Since there's less evaporation in the slow cooker, it uses a lower percentage of liquid in the recipe.

Sweet Potato and Mushroom Risotto

Leaving some liquid in the rice will make it creamier as the butter and Parmesan cheese are stirred in.

makes 2 to 3 servings • hands-on time: 8 min. • total time: 2 hr., 8 min.

2   Tbsp. butter, divided

2   cups peeled sweet potato, cut into 1-inch cubes (1 large)

½   cup refrigerated prechopped onion

¾   cup Arborio rice

½   cup dry white wine

1   (14-oz.) can vegetable broth

1   (8-oz.) package baby portobello mushrooms, quartered

2   tsp. minced fresh thyme

⅔   cup (2½ oz.) shredded Parmesan cheese

½   cup (2 oz.) shredded fontina cheese

1. Melt 1 Tbsp. butter in a large skillet over medium-high heat. Add sweet potato and onion. Cook, stirring often, 3 minutes. Add rice; cook, stirring constantly, 2 minutes. Add wine, stirring to loosen particles from bottom of skillet. Bring to a boil; remove from heat. Transfer rice mixture to a lightly greased 4-qt. slow cooker.

2. Place broth in a microwave-safe bowl. Microwave 1 minute or until hot. Stir broth, mushrooms, and thyme into rice mixture in slow cooker. Cover and cook on HIGH 2 hours or until rice is tender and liquid is almost absorbed.

3. Stir in remaining 1 Tbsp. butter and Parmesan cheese. Sprinkle with fontina cheese.

Mushroom-Stuffed Red Peppers

makes 6 servings • hands-on time: 15 min. • total time: 4 hr., 15 min.

1 cup fire-roasted tomato and garlic pasta sauce

6 medium-size red bell peppers

4 cups coarsely chopped baby portobello mushrooms

½ cup (2 oz.) shredded Parmesan cheese, divided

⅓ cup finely chopped sweet onion

⅓ cup soft, fresh breadcrumbs

1 tsp. chopped fresh thyme

½ tsp. salt

¼ tsp. freshly ground pepper

1 (16-oz.) can navy beans, drained

1 (8.8-oz.) package precooked brown rice

Garnish: fresh thyme

1. Pour pasta sauce into bottom of a 7-qt. oval slow cooker.

2. Cut ½ inch from stem end of each bell pepper. Remove and discard seeds and membranes.

3. Combine mushrooms, ¼ cup cheese, and next 7 ingredients in a large bowl, stirring well. Spoon mushroom mixture into bell peppers. Place peppers in a single layer in slow cooker. Top with remaining ¼ cup cheese. Cover and cook on LOW 4 hours or until peppers are tender. Garnish, if desired.

Mexican Beans and Vegetables with Rice

Picante sauce is a spicy sauce that is similar to salsa. It contributes a great deal of flavor in this veggie-laden dish.

makes 6 servings • hands-on time: 9 min. • total time: 8 hr., 9 min.

⅔   cup picante sauce

1   Tbsp. vegetable oil

1½   tsp. ground cumin

1   tsp. salt

½   tsp. dried oregano

1   (28-oz.) can diced tomatoes, undrained

1   (16-oz.) can red beans, undrained

1   (15-oz.) can black beans, drained and rinsed

1   large onion, chopped

1   large yellow squash or zucchini, cut into ½-inch pieces

1   green bell pepper, cut into ¾-inch pieces

1   red bell pepper, cut into ¾-inch pieces

Hot cooked rice

Garnishes: shredded Cheddar cheese, sour cream, chopped fresh cilantro

1. Stir together first 12 ingredients in a 4-qt. slow cooker. Cover and cook on LOW 8 hours or until vegetables are tender. Serve over hot cooked rice. Garnish, if desired.

ideal slow cooker
4-quart round

Layered Mexican Tortilla Pie

makes 6 to 8 servings • hands-on time: 15 min. • total time: 3 hr., 15 min.

1 Tbsp. canola oil

½ cup refrigerated prechopped onion

1 (12-oz.) package frozen meatless burger crumbles

½ tsp. chili powder

½ tsp. ground cumin

2 (11-oz.) cans yellow corn with red and green bell peppers, drained

Heavy-duty aluminum foil

1 (16-oz.) can refried beans

6 (6-inch) flour tortillas

1⅔ cups fresh salsa

2¾ cups shredded Monterey Jack cheese

Toppings: sour cream, chopped fresh cilantro, shredded Monterey Jack cheese, fresh salsa, guacamole

1. Heat oil in a large nonstick skillet over medium-high heat. Add onion; cook 3 minutes or until tender. Stir in burger crumbles and next 3 ingredients. Cook 2 minutes or until crumbles are thawed. Remove from heat.

2. Fold 2 (17- x 12-inch) sheets of heavy-duty aluminum foil into 2 (17- x 2-inch) strips. Arrange strips in an "X" pattern in a lightly greased 4-qt. round slow cooker, allowing foil to extend 1 inch beyond edges of slow cooker.

3. Spread about ⅓ cup refried beans on each of 5 tortillas. Place 1 tortilla, bean side up, on top of foil X in slow cooker. Spoon 1 cup burger mixture over beans; top with ⅓ cup salsa and ½ cup cheese. Repeat layers 4 times. Top with remaining tortilla, and sprinkle with remaining ¼ cup cheese. Cover and cook on LOW 3 hours or until cheese melts and edges are bubbly.

4. Remove insert from slow cooker; let stand, uncovered, 15 minutes. Grasping ends of foil strips, carefully transfer pie to a serving plate. Carefully remove foil strips. Cut pie into wedges, and serve with desired toppings.

Enchilada Casserole

makes 6 servings • hands-on time: 14 min. • total time: 4 hr., 19 min.

3 Tbsp. diced green chiles, divided

½ cup mild salsa

¼ cup chopped green onions

¼ cup chopped fresh cilantro

1 (15-oz.) can black beans, drained and rinsed

1 (11-oz.) can yellow corn with red and green bell peppers, drained and rinsed

1 (10-oz.) can enchilada sauce

2 large eggs

2 Tbsp. chopped jarred roasted red bell peppers

1 (8½-oz.) package corn muffin mix

1½ cups (6 oz.) shredded Mexican four-cheese blend

Garnish: chopped fresh cilantro

1. Stir together 2 Tbsp. green chiles and next 6 ingredients in a lightly greased 4-qt. slow cooker. Cover and cook on LOW 3 hours.

2. Whisk eggs in a medium bowl; stir in remaining 1 Tbsp. green chiles, roasted bell peppers, and muffin mix. Spoon batter over bean mixture in slow cooker. Cover and cook on LOW 1 hour or until cornbread is done.

3. Sprinkle cheese over cornbread. Increase heat to HIGH; cover and cook 5 minutes or until cheese melts. Spoon into shallow bowls. Garnish, if desired.

Secret Ingredient

Some call it cilantro; others call it coriander, or even Chinese parsley. This native of southern Europe and the Middle East has a pungent flavor, with a faint undertone of anise. One of the most versatile herbs, cilantro adds distinctive flavor to salsas, soups, stews, curries, salads, vegetables, fish, and chicken dishes.

ideal slow cooker
4-quart

Spanish-Style Lentils and Rice

makes 6 to 8 servings • hands-on time: 8 min. • total time: 12 hr., 8 min.

1   cup dried lentils
1   cup uncooked long-grain rice
1   medium onion, chopped
1   medium-size green bell pepper, chopped
2   (14-oz.) cans chicken broth
1   (10-oz.) can diced tomatoes and green chiles
1   tsp. salt
1   tsp. chili powder
½   tsp. ground cumin
¼   tsp. garlic powder
1½   cups (6 oz.) shredded sharp Cheddar cheese

1. Place lentils in a 4-qt. slow cooker. Cover with water 2 inches above lentils; let soak 8 hours. Drain and rinse; return lentils to slow cooker. Add rice and next 8 ingredients.

2. Cover and cook on LOW 4 hours or until lentils and rice are tender. Top with cheese, and serve immediately.

Chunky Minestrone

makes 5 servings • hands-on time: 14 min. • total time: 6 hr., 14 min.

3 (14-oz.) cans low-sodium fat-free chicken broth

2 (14½-oz.) cans no-salt-added diced tomatoes with roasted garlic, undrained

1 (15½-oz.) can cannellini beans, drained and rinsed

1 (10-oz.) package frozen chopped spinach, thawed

1½ cups frozen chopped onion, thawed

1 medium carrot, chopped

1 medium zucchini, quartered and sliced

2 tsp. olive oil

1 tsp. dried Italian seasoning

¼ tsp. freshly ground pepper

½ cup small shell pasta

⅔ cup freshly grated Parmesan cheese

1. Combine first 10 ingredients and 1 cup water in a 4-qt. slow cooker.

2. Cover and cook on LOW 5½ hours. Add pasta, and cook on LOW 30 more minutes. Sprinkle each serving with cheese.

Three-Cheese Broccoli Soup

makes 8 servings • hands-on time: 15 min. • total time: 4 hr., 15 min.

¼ cup butter

1 large onion, chopped

¼ cup all-purpose flour

1 (12-oz.) can evaporated milk

1 (32-oz.) container chicken broth

¼ tsp. salt

½ tsp. freshly ground pepper

1 (14-oz.) package frozen baby broccoli florets

1 (8-oz.) package pasteurized prepared cheese product, cubed

1½ cups (6 oz.) shredded extra-sharp Cheddar cheese

1 cup (4 oz.) shredded Parmesan cheese

Garnish: shredded extra-sharp Cheddar cheese

1. Melt butter in a large skillet over medium-high heat. Add onion. Sauté 4 minutes or until tender. Stir in flour. Cook, stirring constantly, 1 minute. Gradually stir in milk until smooth. Pour milk mixture into a lightly greased 4-qt. slow cooker. Stir in broth and next 3 ingredients. Cover and cook on LOW 4 hours or until bubbly.

2. Add cheese cubes, stirring until cubes melt. Add Cheddar cheese and Parmesan cheese, stirring until cheeses melt. Garnish, if desired. Serve immediately.

Slow-Cooker School

Stirring the cheese cubes into the soup first helps the other cheeses melt more smoothly in the slow cooker when they're added.

Black-eyed Pea Soup

makes 6 to 8 servings   •   hands-on time: 11 min.   •   total time: 20 hr., 11 min.   •   pictured on page 254

1   (16-oz.) package dried black-eyed peas

6   bacon slices

1   (8-oz.) container refrigerated prechopped onion

1   medium-size red bell pepper, chopped

1   (48-oz.) container chicken broth

1   Tbsp. jarred minced garlic

1   (14½-oz.) can diced tomatoes and zesty mild green chiles, undrained

Garnish: chopped green onions

1. Rinse and sort peas according to package directions. Place peas in a Dutch oven. Cover with water 2 inches above peas; let soak 8 hours. Drain. Place peas in a 6-qt. slow cooker.

2. Cook bacon in a large skillet over medium-high heat 5 to 7 minutes or until crisp; remove bacon, and drain on paper towels, reserving drippings in skillet. Coarsely crumble bacon.

3. Add onion to drippings in skillet; cook, stirring constantly, 4 minutes or until tender. Stir bacon, onion, bell pepper, and next 3 ingredients into peas in slow cooker. Cover and cook on LOW 12 hours or until peas are tender. Garnish, if desired.

Vegetable Tortellini Soup

makes 6 servings • hands-on time: 5 min. • total time: 7 hr., 23 minutes

Cooking spray

2 (8-oz.) packages refrigerated prechopped celery, onion, and bell pepper mix

½ tsp. pepper

1 medium zucchini, coarsely chopped

1 (32-oz.) container chicken broth

1 (16-oz.) package frozen baby corn, bean, pea, and carrot mix

1 (15½-oz.) can cannellini beans, drained and rinsed

1 (14½-oz.) can diced tomatoes with basil, oregano, and garlic, undrained

1 (9-oz.) package refrigerated cheese tortellini

Garnish: shredded Parmesan cheese

1. Heat a large nonstick skillet over medium-high heat. Coat pan with cooking spray. Add celery mixture, and sauté 5 minutes or until tender. Transfer mixture to a 5-qt. slow cooker. Stir in pepper and next 5 ingredients. Cover and cook on LOW 7 hours.

2. Increase heat to HIGH; add tortellini. Cover and cook 18 minutes or until pasta is tender. Garnish, if desired.

ideal slow cooker
5-quart

Moroccan Lentil Stew

makes 8 servings • hands-on time: 11 min. • total time: 8 hr., 11 min.

1   cup dried lentils
2   cups refrigerated cubed peeled
      butternut squash
1   cup sliced carrot
2   tsp. ground turmeric
1   tsp. ground ginger
¼   tsp. salt
½   tsp. freshly ground pepper
½   tsp. ground cinnamon
Pinch of saffron threads
2   (14½-oz.) cans diced tomatoes,
      undrained
1   large onion, chopped
3   garlic cloves, minced

1. Rinse and sort lentils according to package directions. Stir together lentils, squash, 2 cups water, and remaining ingredients in a 5-qt. slow cooker. Cover and cook on LOW 8 hours.

Secret Ingredient

Butternut squash adds a sweet and nutty flavor to this stew. Of all the winter squashes, butternut squash is the easiest to work with; it has thin skin and can be peeled easily with a vegetable peeler. Its dense flesh and robust flavor work well in a variety of dishes, from sweet to savory. Look for cubed peeled butternut squash in the produce section of your supermarket to make the prep for this recipe a snap.

ideal slow cooker
6-quart

Cinnamon-Pecan Breakfast Bread Pudding

Prepare the topping at the same time as the bread mixture so it will be ready to sprinkle on when it's time to cook the pudding.

makes 5 servings • hands-on time: 12 min. • total time: 12 hr., 42 min.

5 Tbsp. butter, divided
1 (16-oz.) loaf French bread, cut into ½-inch-thick slices
1½ cups sugar, divided
4 tsp. ground cinnamon, divided
¼ tsp. ground nutmeg
8 large eggs
3 cups half-and-half
2 Tbsp. vanilla extract
2 Tbsp. all-purpose flour
1 cup coarsely chopped pecans

1. Grease a 6-qt. slow cooker with 1 Tbsp. butter. Arrange bread slices in bottom of slow cooker. Whisk together ¾ cup sugar, 3 tsp. cinnamon, and nutmeg. Whisk in eggs, half-and-half, and vanilla. Pour over bread. Cover and chill at least 8 hours or up to 18 hours.

2. Whisk together remaining ¾ cup sugar, remaining 1 tsp. cinnamon, and flour in a bowl. Cut in remaining 4 Tbsp. butter until crumbly; stir in pecans. Cover and chill until ready to use.

3. Remove bread mixture from refrigerator. Sprinkle pecan mixture over bread mixture. Cover and cook on HIGH 1 hour. Reduce heat to LOW; cover and cook 3½ hours or until puffed and set.

Metric Equivalents

The information in the following charts is provided to help cooks outside the United States successfully use the recipes in this book. All equivalents are approximate.

EQUIVALENTS FOR DIFFERENT TYPES OF INGREDIENTS

Standard Cup	Fine Powder (ex. flour)	Grain (ex. rice)	Granular (ex. sugar)	Liquid Solids (ex. butter)	Liquid (ex. milk)
1	140 g	150 g	190 g	200 g	240 ml
¾	105 g	113 g	143 g	150 g	180 ml
⅔	93 g	100 g	125 g	133 g	160 ml
½	70 g	75 g	95 g	100 g	120 ml
⅓	47 g	50 g	63 g	67 g	80 ml
¼	35 g	38 g	48 g	50 g	60 ml
⅛	18 g	19 g	24 g	25 g	30 ml

LIQUID INGREDIENTS BY VOLUME

¼ tsp =			1 ml
½ tsp =			2 ml
1 tsp =			5 ml
3 tsp =	1 Tbsp =	½ fl oz =	15 ml
	2 Tbsp = ⅛ cup =	1 fl oz =	30 ml
	4 Tbsp = ¼ cup =	2 fl oz =	60 ml
	5⅓ Tbsp = ⅓ cup =	3 fl oz =	80 ml
	8 Tbsp = ½ cup =	4 fl oz =	120 ml
	10⅔ Tbsp = ⅔ cup =	5 fl oz =	160 ml
	12 Tbsp = ¾ cup =	6 fl oz =	180 ml
	16 Tbsp = 1 cup =	8 fl oz =	240 ml
	1 pt = 2 cups =	16 fl oz =	480 ml
	1 qt = 4 cups =	32 fl oz =	960 ml
		33 fl oz =	1000 ml = 1 l

DRY INGREDIENTS BY WEIGHT

(To convert ounces to grams, multiply the number of ounces by 30.)

1 oz =	¹⁄₁₆ lb =	30 g
4 oz =	¼ lb =	120 g
8 oz =	½ lb =	240 g
12 oz =	¾ lb =	360 g
16 oz =	1 lb =	480 g

LENGTH

(To convert inches to centimeters, multiply the number of inches by 2.5.)

1 in =		2.5 cm
6 in =	½ ft =	15 cm
12 in =	1 ft =	30 cm
36 in =	3 ft = 1 yd =	90 cm
40 in =		100 cm = 1 m

COOKING/OVEN TEMPERATURES

	Fahrenheit	Celsius	Gas Mark
Freeze Water	32° F	0° C	
Room Temperature	68° F	20° C	
Boil Water	212° F	100° C	
Bake	325° F	160° C	3
	350° F	180° C	4
	375° F	190° C	5
	400° F	200° C	6
	425° F	220° C	7
	450° F	230° C	8
Broil			Grill

Index